if i had to tell it again

if i had to tell it again

A Memoir

gayathri prabhu

HarperCollins *Publishers* India

First published in India by
HarperCollins *Publishers* in 2017

HarperCollins Publishers India, Cyber City, Building 10-A, Gurugram,
Haryana-122002, India
www.harpercollins.co.in

2 4 6 8 10 9 7 5 3 1

P-ISBN: 978-93-5277-375-6
E-ISBN: 978-93-5277-376-3

Typeset in 12/15 Adobe Garamond Pro at
SURYA, New Delhi

Printed and bound at
MicroPrints India, New Delhi

MIX
Paper
FSC FSC® C218906

This product is made of FSC®-certified and other controlled material.

HarperCollins Publishers, Macken House, 39/40 Mayor Street
Upper, Dublin 1, D01 C9W8, Ireland

In memoriam

S.G.M. Prabhu
(1948–2014)

and

Chinna
(2002–2015)

If I Had to Tell It Again

That night my phone battery dies. Its charger has been forgotten in the office, so the phone remains dead. I sleep deeply. The other phone in the house rings. It is my sister. Dense sleep, garbled speech and something about our ill father. I wake slowly. I have spoken to him two hours ago – not spoken, argued as always. For he never listens to us, or to reason. He is ill, scheduled to travel to Manipal in the morning, to get admitted to the hospital here. This call is about him. I hear voices in the background. My brother-in-law speaking on another phone. 'Akka, I think he is dead,' she says. I'll never forget her voice, the muffled shock, the tremors of pain. Inside me, something is released. Finally.

An hour later, at 2 a.m., I am in a taxi, just me and the driver, someone I have never met before. A few polite words have to be exchanged as I settle down in the front seat. We are headed for Mysore. My phone is still dead, no voices can reach me, and my voice speaks only to me. I have been preparing myself for this day since I was barely a teenager, when my father had started to speak out his death wish, and he had wished for death repeatedly since then. He had been so deeply unhappy with his life, so given to substance abuse to numb out his inability to cope, and I had probably made up my mind to let him go, a million times in the passing years, I had imagined his death till it had come to mean just something to get over with.

Die, why don't you just die? Why threaten, why not do something about it? I would say this to my father, part exasperation, part dark humour, and he would laugh aloud at my impudence. It was all a joke.

Not night, not morning, not even dawn, but some indeterminate grey hour. The car slowly makes its way up the steep, bumpy curves of a dark hillside. Just silence and moonlight and the headlights of our car for a while, till our solitude is interrupted by the lights of a passing vehicle, and then, silence and moonlight restored, we sit beside each other, the driver and I, quiet strangers. The stately silhouettes of the Western Ghats in the moonlight, moving around us, round and round. I indicate that we need to stop. My feet touch earth. My stomach overturns. The driver hands me some water,

I mumble thanks. We get back in the car, hurrying to Mysore. But why hurry, he is already dead, he would stay dead.

Few dawns would compare to the sheer beauty of this one. The silhouettes are now fleshed. The greens stirring to life on the mountains. A mauve sheen across the skies. A shy infant sun.

That moment stays with me, not the sight of the dead father, or the tears in the eyes of my mother and sister when I finally reach Mysore in the morning. I have no tears to offer him – they had all dried up long ago. I had just wanted him gone, hadn't I? And he did keep his word, even if it took him two decades to drink his liver to death. I had sworn in his hearing that I would not cry when he died, not a drop, for I was sick of bearing the weight of such a father.

That moment in the car, a shaking, moving moment, stays with me. More real, stronger somehow, than the four decades of knowing this father.

My father fantasized constantly about death. It was his lover, his great affair, and not so secret either. It should be quick, he would say, I believe in Lord Ganesha and he will not let me suffer. I will not be a burden on any of you. I will go quickly. All this he would say again and again. I just want to die, I just want to die, oh when will I die …

That bottle of Rum, always Old Monk, all through my teenage years it was a bottle every night. The last few years, he was drinking in the afternoons too. Two bottles now. I could not bear to be around him. I felt repulsion, anger, frustration.

It was impossible to convince him to turn his face to life instead of craving death, so one agreed with him, to fortify and manifest his desire. Go when you must.

It was only months after his death that I understood his fantasy about death had no room for thoughts about dying. I had not thought about it either. Death, he wanted, but dying had terrified him, and neither of us had been prepared for that.

Sixteen weeks before he died, he had been diagnosed with liver cirrhosis. How bad is it, we all wanted to know from the doctor. Hard to say, but no more drinking, and get treatment for the symptoms. He may have days or he may have a decade, the doctor had said, as I hurried to match pace through the hospital corridor, it depends on his luck, entirely his luck.

Luck.

The one thing my father mourned he never had. Unlucky in everything, he had said. For many years. He believed it deeply too. Unlucky. Unlucky. And a failure, he constantly labelled himself. Finally something was happening just the way he had hoped.

Luck.

What are you going to do about it, my sister and I had asked him after he had come back from the hospital.

He knew what we meant. Was he going to be sensible? Was he finally going to listen to us? Was he going to get expert opinion, the best treatment?

I'll do it my way, he snapped. As always.

And as always we were resigned. My sister, good soldier, tried to argue. But I had taught myself to see it like he did. We had had years, him and me, to sort this out, hadn't we? This death craving of his, which he had bequeathed to me, turning me into its custodian while I was still a child, was how I had survived this father. Barely.

In the days that had followed, as we went through the initial treatment, as he gave up drinking, something unexpected surfaced. First hesitant, then audacious, then plaintive: a desire to live. I was shocked, betrayed. How could he go back on the great dramatic moment he had orchestrated for years? How could he?

He had prepared me for his death, but not for this turn to life.

I had developed no intuition for this new terrain, nor did I have the time. There was work, household, the routine of getting through the weeks. Sixteen weeks later he was dead.

Sixty-six years of a lifetime gone.

There would be no funeral. He had donated his body to the local medical college. It was part of his script, his fantasy about death. He would show his hospital donation certificate to anyone who came to our house. No rituals for me, he would announce. To his mind there was some justice in being cut up by medical students. He had wanted to be a doctor. We had heard that story many times – the dream that had to be sacrificed for his family responsibilities – but of course he had been unlucky.

There is his corpse, lying on the floor, people constantly milling around, talking about his untimely, unfortunate death, while I stare at everyone in dry-eyed annoyance. He had always been a popular man, much loved, generous to a fault to his neighbours, even if angry towards his own family. I just want him gone from the house. When the van from the morgue comes to pick him up, everyone urges us to touch his feet, to ask for his blessings. It is expected from children of dead parents. Everyone watches us.

You first, an old man points to me, my father's first-born.

I bend down, my fingers touch his feet.

In my mind the words form, loud and distinct – I forgive you.

~

When a child grows up with an angry, frustrated, depressive parent, there is only a shadow of the human-parent, the rest is just dark unfathomable weight. And then one gets used to it.

The dead man's bed has to be burnt, the pillow too, someone says, and we mutely nod. Sure, take it out, burn it.

He vomited so much blood, my mother said later, the night he died. I know how much he loved the dramatic, the melodramatic, and this would have been a story he would have narrated with much relish. Every little bloody detail.

There is blood splattered here and there. In the bathroom, a bloodied bed sheet soaks in a bucket of red water.

Sure, take that bed, burn it down.

On the bare cot, bereft of the mattress, is a diary, a dark green diary. It had been tucked under his pillow.

Can I take it?

Yes, take it.

How could I not want it? I am the writer in the family, the inheritor of my father's storytelling compulsion.

What's in the diary?

Nobody has the energy to find out. But I give it a quick glance. Writing in those bold rounded letters that are so familiar, though they had turned shaky, often illegible. Fragmented writings, poems and inspirational quotes, some by famous thinkers, some anonymous. He had made such jottings for decades. Nearly all in the Kannada script, a collection of inspiring or interesting proverbs and quotes. It is not new information and nothing more is asked or said about the diary.

This is what he wrote and read when he was ill, when he tried hard not to think about dying, when even the death he wanted was no longer spoken of. He had courted life – I can see it in the sporadic writing in that green diary, most of the pages still blank. Not only did he not want to die, he wanted to get better, he believed there was a better self, a better world. Who is this man? A stranger to me, my very own dusty mirror.

This green diary will accuse me forever. I had had absolutely no compassion for a dying father. And I had felt reluctant to be drawn into his new script, his shirking away from that promised exit.

The diary comes home with me, tightly shut,

awaiting its reader, another day, another year, another life perhaps.

I forgive you.

But how?

~

The story of depression is hard to tell, always in fragments, hard to cast in words, hard to tell when it seeped out of him, into and through me. Like that legacy of storytelling.

He was always telling stories, embellishing every narrative, introducing dramatic interludes, enacting scenes, inviting laughter and comments, as if on a stage, as if in a spotlight. My father, the showman, revelled in repetition, in amplifying details to the elastic limits of credibility. Some of these stories I had heard more times than I can count. No two tellings were alike, and yet every telling felt like the most plausible, most immediate, such was his gift.

An artist. An aesthete.

To a child, to me, he seemed infallible and his talents inexhaustible. He sang, he danced, he drummed, he could draw and craft beautiful objects, he created gardens from weeds, and he was the raconteur of the human race. There was nothing he could not fix –

broken chairs, fused circuits, clogged pipes, cranky machines – and his children were the keepers of an elaborate box of tools, his handy assistants.

Our mother, gentle and hesitant, paled into the landscape of my childhood. She was the alcove to our father's durbar.

He was everything I thought I aspired to be, before we grappled with teenage, before he concluded that the curve of his life would only dip, never rise. And because he had declared himself a failure, there was no room for me to be anything but a success. His performing monkey, I would say bitterly as an adult. But then, at ten, it was simply what one did. Please a father. He loved to see his child perform, he ached for others to praise the child, he waited eagerly for every prize the child could bring home and then show it around to everyone.

So intense was the love, bordering on obsession, for this first-born who had to undo the failings of his life, that its other side had to be rage. Invariably.

Surely there must have been demons in his head. He had twenty-six years before I was born, years that must have been steeped in humiliations, disappointments, heartbreak. Hadn't he been raw and sensitive? Hadn't he been naïve and trusting? Always the most entertaining in a gathering, hadn't his loneliness over the unsharable, his agony over lost dreams been crushing?

Why else would he explode into that white, frothy fury? Why else would his hand rise to strike at the smallest provocation? Why else would the leather belt around his waist end up in his hands, then fall on our backs? Why else would there be brutal thrashings inside locked, lightless rooms while our mother banged pitifully on the door from outside? Beatings, not till lessons were learnt but till his arms tired. More punishment followed every tear shed, for tears were unbearable to him, never mind our pain.

So blinding was that fury, so close to the surface, blinding him and us. Intense anger.

And then intense love. Soon after the beatings, the rage also beaten out of him, he would return to the room to cuddle and fuss over our little bodies.

Love and anger. Perhaps the difference was not evident to him till the end. An hour before he died, he was on the phone fighting with both his children.

Forgiveness is a complicated affair.

There was that time when I was thirty years old, working on my second novel, when the fiction beneath my typing fingers mined deeper sorrows. I wrote about my protagonist who had a physically abusive mother, I wrote about how that pain spawns more pain endlessly, how it can never heal, I wrote till rivulets of tears ran dry. Then I picked up the phone, called my father, heard him talk about neighbourhood intrigues, said nothing till the final bye, my silence going unnoticed, then put my head on the computer keyboard and cried as though it was my first cry. Until then I had not seen the big knot of wrath and sorrow inside me for what had been endured. How come it had taken me so long to know that anger was not just his domain, it had been strapped to my back too? Love did not absolve violence – about that I was a late learner.

~

Dead people need to tell their stories. And he has spun so many, that some can be recreated here, ever so briefly, without the daughter's lens.

The world according to SGM:

He has had the worst luck, no two ways about it, and everybody he loves deeply has eventually failed him …

He can barely tolerate his wife, the most selfish person he knows, and the reason he has to escape, but not through the cowardice of suicide, just heroic, silent submersion in alcohol …

Nobody understands him, and even though there is nothing he believes in more than the innate goodness of the world, good people are scarce in the world and everything in a state of irrevocable decline …

He is an unlucky man, a failure, and all he wants is a swift death …

But wait.

Long before this narrative of drink and desperation, there was another father.

Take Two. The world according to a youthful SGM:

He was born in a coastal village, one among many siblings, witness to a stormy equation between his parents, for which he always held his mother responsible, almost with hostility. He would have been lost in the sea of children of that household, were it not for his grandfather who saw his own chutzpah replicated in the little boy and doted on him. But when the old man died, he had to learn to love himself, and this was very difficult to do in a place where people spoke bluntly, where expressions of affections were infrequent and considered unnecessary.

He was marked to be that strange creature: a gregarious loner. He wanted to be wanted, stand out in every gathering, but only to make sure everyone noticed his profound loneliness. That trait would stay with him till the end.

He wanted to be a doctor but family responsibilities held him back in the village. And when he did end up in college, it was to study accounts and commerce. But never mind, he surely thought, he would find his own way in the world, he would fill it with his own vitality, his faith in friendship, his laughter and chatter. He saw the world as a place milling with bright people who deserved unconditional trust. When he could, he acted in plays, sang songs, and always, always made friends.

Surrounded by clansmen whose trading ancestry had turned 'practical' into a haloed word, where youngsters walked away from family shops to get into steady jobs in medicine, engineering, banking or chartered accountancy, his secret was his untapped artistry.

He would find a job in a bank, even if it was that of a clerk, and he would make his way up. Somewhere in those eventful early twenties, there came romance, a matching of hearts, but it would end prematurely. After that came a marriage, arranged by the will of elders and the matching of horoscopes, but it was not a marriage of temperaments.

Much hinges on the story of this marriage, hard for a child to narrate, a flawed witness by every count. If the wife were to tell this story, she might be able to talk about the strain of being married to a man who lived by his passion and not by his prudence, about the flares of physical and verbal violence, the dominating presence that brooded, the money troubles, the drinking, the drinking ...

But this story has to be his, and he would not see it his wife's way. Never.

And this has long ceased to be the account of a youthful, non-depressive SGM, so I can try again.

Take Three. If SGM's life had to be put into a colourful brochure, full of golden light and cherubic smiles:

It would be a story of triumph, of a boy born just a year after Indian independence, a first-generation college graduate, making the move from a remote village in coastal Karnataka to a bustling town. There wasn't much money or support from the family, but nor was there any expectation that he would return to live with them. An untethered flight. As the seventies arrived, the circumstances were right for him to turn away from the family trade. Some of the top banks in the country, all owned by private individuals, had been nationalized in one swift move by Indira Gandhi, and the little clerical job he had was open to many possibilities. He got to travel, see different parts of the country, his responsibilities to his parental hearth were taken care of early, even as his own family grew. He had found just the sort of wife he wanted, the docile kind who would stay at home and take care of his needs, and his children were daughters, just as he wanted, and they learnt their lessons from him quickly enough. There was also a white furry dog that was with the family for nearly two decades, that he loved to distraction. He had a regular source of income, a house that he owned, innumerable friends who adored him – everything seemed in place for a peaceful, happy retirement.

Wrong Take.

It never worked out like that, and nothing of that brochure narrative seemed to be good outcomes to him.

Retain Take One.

He would say the intoxicants saved him. The chewing tobacco, the alcohol, and for a few years, cigarettes too. How could he possibly have managed otherwise? He worked so hard, harder than anyone around him – he poured his everything into his work, but did not know how to deal with the fact that not everyone was as earnest and selfless. He never understood that too much honesty, too much hard work and too much trust in strangers were bound to be perilous.

The world was already a damaged place and he could not see how imperfect his notion of perfection was.

People would come into grace and then fall out of it. The only thing that stayed constant, that gave him some release from the dark shadows in his head was the drink, quite watery in the early years, then dense bitterness straight from the bottle.

Two people first saw the signs of occasional drinking turning into inescapable alcoholism – he and I.

I was a schoolgirl, he was a stressed overworked bank manager, and between us was the bottle.

Hide it, he would insist, and no matter what I say, don't give it to me.

I would nod solemnly, determined not to let him down.

Please, please, where is that bottle I gave you? Give it to me. Just one peg, just one peg, I promise.

Which father should I have listened to? The one who was spiralling into addiction or the one who needed alcohol to make it through one more night, one more day?

It was a great burden on someone barely a teenager. A great guilt too. Love was to be my undoing as much as his. I always resisted the nightly pleadings, but invariably I would give in. The one helping would vanish. More pleadings.

Fine, one more swig.

You pour it, he would say.

My hands would tremble, my heart cold.

If this was the road to our family's doom, I was sending him that way, or so it felt. His desperation was always there, intensely visceral.

Was there ever a father I could count on? I don't know. If there was one such father, that was the year he must have receded, faded away.

Love, our undoing. So much love. It was love that manifested in the strangest ways. In fear, in pride, in violence, in encouragement, in neglect, in drink. If I could change one thing of those lost years, it would be to be loved less by him. For my sister, it might just be the other way round – it might be an excavation for love.

~

Not having a son, my father had been told all his life, would doom the Brahmin male soul. Who would deliver it to the other world? Daughters didn't count. With typical irreverence, he had instructed that no rituals be conducted before his corpse was sent off to the medical college.

My mother had mixed feelings about all this. She liked custom and tradition.

I'll be a ghost, dangle from a tree, he had joked repeatedly, and she had tried to laugh with him.

As it turned out, after his death, the disposal of the body and leave-taking ceremonies were the last thing on our minds.

I am relieved, my mother kept saying, that it was not

suicide. He talked about killing himself more and more frequently towards the end. Anything but a suicide, my mother said. Suicide was the greatest crime and his soul would never get deliverance. The soul would have suffered, stayed a burden on earth. Every day I thank God, she said, that it was not a suicide.

What else was it? This drinking till the liver collapsed, till there was bleeding in the throat, in the intestines, bleeding from every orifice. His O+ve blood, same as mine, that he had donated so many times to save lives, spilling out of him. Blood in his stools, blood in his vomit, blood on the bedroom floor, blood in the car that rushed him to the hospital, blood in the emergency room of the two hospitals they took him to, so much blood that they had put him in the deep freezer to stem the flow. For days after he was dead, our eyes would alight on stray specks of blood on a bathroom tile, on some cloth, on one edge of the sink where I stood brushing my teeth.

The self-deception of her no-suicide relief was lost on my mother.

We were exhausted. The body was gone. All the visitors had left. We sat around the dining table, mother and two daughters, eating takeaway from a nearby restaurant, talking about the foolishness of this dead man who had decided to get treatment too late.

You are now a free woman, I told my mother. For years he threatened to go, and now he is gone. Now you can live your life.

She sniffled into the edge of her sari, saying, how could he do this to me? Never listened to me, followed everybody's advice but mine.

He is gone, I reminded her, and you are free.

A dead man's soul stays on earth, stays in his house, for twelve days after the body is cold, my mother said.

I doubt it. He was in a hurry to go, always, wanting to die early, swiftly, without hospital stays or lingering illness. Did he anticipate what our lives would be without him? His green diary, the one found under his pillow, now rests in the clutter of my bag. How can I possibly open it, read it? Not yet.

Three days later, we are in my father's old car, my sister and I. She is driving me to the railway station. We had decided she would stay on for a fortnight to help my mother, and then it would be my turn in the summer to sort out the paperwork.

My father's daughters, united by a deep fondness for each other, were divided by his erratic ways.

When we were growing up, when he was alive, we both knew we were not the same for him. I was the darling, the doted-on, and she was the afterthought, the ignored. Both roads were equally hard with this man.

I remember every single slap, every thrashing, every yelling. And I remember feeling unworthy, unimportant, fraught. My sister remembers almost nothing, but knows she was punished, treated unfairly. Everything has been blocked out, barricaded, everything but the resentment. Two children, born of the same parents and living in the same house, enduring nearly the same punishments – one suffers from not remembering and the other from remembering too much. Such are the workings of trauma.

Between us are seen and unseen battle lines.

He always loved you more, she says.

The streets of Mysore are almost deserted, winding down and soothingly quiet. The street lamps cast big pools of light on the gentle grey of the road, the familiar road. So quiet, so cool, those stray April winds.

I have heard this a million times. I was his favourite. He loved me very much.

And I am weary of being apologetic for it. His love has been a chain around my neck, my feet – it had almost killed me. And she would never see it my way. Why should she? Her version is just as real, just as consuming.

It was bloody hard being his favourite, and the price I paid was too high, I say aloud.

She listens, hands on the wheel, eyes on the road.

Anointed the unfailing sidekick to his mercurial act, one had to be perfect, always gather praise, always succeed. And be thrashed with anything he could lay his hands on when disappointed. He had tethered me early to his views on what to be and do in the world, not an ounce of coping skill taught or put in place. Look what he did, constantly putting me in unsafe situations, because people are all good and supposed to admire me like he did. But it never occurred to him that I was just a child, accessible. It was exhausting, damaging, infuriating to be his favourite. Probably just as bad as being the ignored child, like you – difficult in a different way, but difficult nonetheless.

It was difficult for you.

For the first time, I hear her acknowledge my perspective on our childhood, agree without even the flicker of hesitation. For the very first time. It is an extraordinary feeling for me. Almost of levitation.

And then something else feels extraordinary.

A shape in my awareness. Just like our father. There in the car, in the back seat, I feel he is listening to us.

He is here, listening, I tell my sister.

I hope he heard everything, she says.

I nod. It is another car ride I will never forget.

Good riddance, I say.

~

There are holes in this story and it looks like a sieve.

Not because I forget, but because the holes fascinate me more than the woven strands around them.

He was the consummate weaver, the finest storyteller I knew. And I was the gatherer of the gaps, the unspoken. He loved to talk, and he knew how to work an audience. His stories dot my childhood like wild flowers across a meadow.

I remember them all.

It made me want to tell stories too. It made me a writer.

He was unprepared for the seriousness with which I withdrew into the cave of my craft, blinds pulled down to the lights of his world.

All he had was one plan, one expectation, and it had packed up – there was nothing else to take its place. The plan was to incubate success, a daughter with accomplishments, enough to impress the many people who gravitated to him. He prided himself on the fact that he did not raise us to be conventional girls – we were told to have careers, follow our dreams, always be exceptional. There was never any pressure to get married, and he proudly sent us to distant cities for our higher studies. In return, he wanted to hear the applause, the accolades. But my life trajectory defied him.

He wanted me to be a television journalist, watched and admired by the world every single day. I freelanced on odd media jobs, I sometimes stayed unemployed, and then I wrote two novels that went unnoticed.

He wanted me to be the poster child for the warrior talk he spouted but could not live himself. I cracked open when I was thirty-one. Broken marriage and clinical depression like eggshells under my feet.

He wanted me to always surge forward, fly upwards. I returned to studies at a time when my friends were sending their children to school. I restarted life from two suitcases when others my age were buying their houses.

He watched me through the grey of his gloom. Soon I was nearing forty, no debt but no savings either, back under his roof as a single woman with a doctorate but no job. And when the teaching job did come, it seemed on par with being a writer nobody read – nothing to fuss about.

In the last years, I noticed his eyes rarely stayed on me, for they were heavy with one question. How could it have gone so wrong? This was the repository of all his hopes – his beautiful, chirpy child of promise. Her hair had greyed in her youth, she had grown quieter, retreated into some secret uncommunicative furrow where there was no room for the father once adulated.

Perhaps, he thought and said aloud, he had raised us all wrong. All that freedom, what good did it do? There is a reason why men are men and women are women and why all those gender roles must be upheld – it is a mistake to think one can raise girls like boys. That is why it had gone so wrong.

He tried to backtrack but it was too late. Life had already taught his daughters that freedom is not something one 'gives' – it stays nestled in each person. And if at all there is any giving of freedom, there is no taking it back, certainly not the notion, the deep taste of it, not even when the taste is acrid.

I was twelve or so, my sister trailing behind me by three years and nine months, and we had just moved to the biggest city I had seen. Having figured out which school we should attend, my father put us both on a school bus and handed me money for enrolment. It was an unending bus journey with imagined fears at the other end of it. We were soon in our new school, the only children in a long queue of parents. I had to pay the fees, find my sister's classroom for her and then figure out my own. Somewhere in that day was one limpid moment when adulthood exploded in my head. I was unsure if I could ever expect my father to do things for me after that.

I never did.

Like the time I missed a train, my first long train journey away from home, standing on the platform, late in the night, in a city I do not know, alone …

Like the time I woke up in the middle of the night desperate for a drink of water, the night after a surgery, in too much pain to crawl out of bed, alone …

Like the time I had no roof to call my own, my entire life stuffed into two suitcases, dragging them across the city, in and out of buses, up three flights of stairs, alone …

If our father did not come to the rescue, it was because he believed in spines toughened by hardships. (There is little that daunts me now, that cannot be denied.) The whipping we received had the same rationale. He had grandly announced he would stop hitting us when we became teenagers, and mostly he stayed true to his word. That was also when the drinking increased, as if the rage had to be gulped down.

You turned out fine *because* of the disciplining, he always said.

We turned out fine *despite* you – much of our adult energy was expended in communicating that to our father.

Before the alcoholism, we did not have the language to tell our truth.

Afterwards, the alcoholism did not carry our words to him.

~

Such a great man, your father, and as a writer you are obliged to write a book about his many accomplishments – this was said to us by his friends who had dropped in to pay condolences.

Write of his greatness?

A genuinely selfless man, they said, always working tirelessly for others.

True. The children in the local orphanage grieved when they found out he had died. He would go there with a cake on every child's birthday. He listened to their chatter, regaled them with tales, helped them as much as he could. While those children wept for him, my father's daughters were mostly dry-eyed. We had been exhausted by his generosity and greatness.

Here was a man who had saved no money but gave to anyone who appeared to be in need. He grumbled about the smallest chore in his house but rushed to slave for others without a second thought. Roadside trees had to be watered, all the stray dogs in the neighbourhood fed, every passer-by's well-being inquired after. All his life, his face had been turned outwards, looking to the world, hungry for love and sympathy, so hungry, and perhaps what his family gave had seemed gravely inadequate.

Did he leave wanting – wanting more?

The rhetoric of sacrifice and self-denial was our father's mainstay. We were told to refuse all favours, give rather than take, and always say no, especially when in want. We never asked for anything as children or we shook our heads furiously in refusal – it was our only hope of a stray windfall.

No. No. No.

A self-made man – one of the visitors was echoing the praise my father valued the most.

Nothing had been taken from the ancestors. SGM hated to take gifts, refused family land or produce, lived entirely on his earnings. He had often bragged about this mythic making of the self.

And fearless, they said.

Remember the time he had all his teeth extracted over one weekend? Not just the rotted teeth but the ones that would rot in the future as well. A man of courage, everyone agreed.

Yes, you should write about what a great man he was.

I was quiet, obviously a rude, unfeeling girl.

But what can I say to these friends of his, these RSS workers? I find it hard to agree with them on anything. I find it hard to believe there is a saffron flag flying on top of my father's house. It was around Hindutva politics that we had had our first real fight, over the whole Ayodhya agenda of the BJP, when I was a teenager. My father has never voted for any other party and harboured a virulent animosity for all members of one religion. After the initial storms of disagreements, we had rarely discussed politics, mostly because it drove him crazy that I did not see things his way.

The visitors left after an eternity of tea and small talk. If I wrote all I knew about my father, nobody would believe me. He had told his life story so many times and with such virtuosity that my version can only be a feeble echo. But these echoes are all we have, as we learn to live without him.

~

My father never acknowledged his vortex of darkness as depression. He said it was genuine suffering caused by his life's unfortunate circumstances and that nobody in the world understood him. It was only for a few years that drinking seemed to give him explicit pleasure. After that the undiluted rum was gulped as though it were medicine, and in the last years he would grimace hard and force the liquid down his gullet. Tortured and inexorable, that's how his drinking looked.

We were not short of causalities or excuses for this, some specific, others existential: he took voluntary retirement from his job in his early fifties and the unemployment was too much to handle; the plans he made for a business of his own, or for voluntary work, never quite took off and there was plenty of time to drink in the day; his marriage and his wife were dragging him down; the dog he loved more than anybody else had to be put to sleep after many months of terminal illness; his mother was bedridden in her nineties and taking care of her for a few months drove him out of his mind; he and his wife were in a road accident a couple of years before his death (she recovered from her head injury but his index finger was irreparably damaged); he was frightened of his own approaching old age, of the possibility of any disability or dependence.

Always some explanation, none of which matters now. All we had to do was name and accept the illness.

It was hard. We were swamped, I found, by the judgement of those who could bear to have anything to do with mental illness or depression. How could a fractured mind, already suffering, endure that? We begged our father to seek help, but he would not. I just want to die, he said, don't worry, I won't be a burden on you.

Ten years ago, just when I had thought I had become my own person, purged of many of my father's traits, and was floating on the open seas in my own style, untethered to him, it came knocking on my door. And it looked familiar. It was what he had refused to name, and it was now with me.

I called it whatever the doctor called it, went to therapy, took my medication, clawed my way out, inch by inch, over many years.

My father called my struggles a sign of weakness – nothing at all like that brave drink-soaked angst of his.

I pointed out that he did not have the stomach for a good fight, like I did. Look, my fists were always curled, I was always in the ring, I stayed up for every single round. He was the one making poor choices, in people, in substances – I was speaking more and more bluntly as I aged. What was there to fear, after the worst came and went?

Perhaps I could have helped him. But I did not. Deliberately, I stayed angry, I stayed critical. I left no lines of connection open. To me, retrieving him from a condition that he refused to acknowledge, that he insisted on escalating, was not just futile but likely to harm my own recovery. Eventually, when his spirit wanted to live, his body began to rapidly fail, and I avoided him as much as possible. I was withdrawn, curt, rolled tight, like a snail.

Four months before his death, we were just back from the hospital, with all the cirrhosis confirmations in a file, and he was surprisingly pliant. He stopped drinking, took the medicines he had been given and followed the diet prescribed. He looked at us like he had never had a single self-destructive thought in his life. He even muttered something about liver transplants. Who was this man? It was maddening.

And when I did try to do something right, it came out all wrong.

Learn to behave like a daughter, he said over something inconsequential, and do as I tell you.

I will behave like a daughter if you behave like a father, but you have never known how, I shouted back.

He blamed my independence. I blamed him. He blamed himself for instilling a taste for rebellion in us. It was a customary deadlock.

Go away. Get out. I don't need anyone. His voice was

trembling, his knuckles swaying dangerously between us, his eyes bloodshot. I won't be around for too long, I want to die.

I will go away. And please do die. I promise you I will not shed a single tear if you die.

All this shouting happened during our last meeting. We had forgotten how to love and all that remained in the last few years was a terrific hunger for confrontation. We spoke but we did not listen. We yelled into the walls. What did we gain?

If I had to tell it again, I would do it like this.

~

True, you were not perfect.

But hey, look at me – I am talking to a dead man.

Are all monologues foredoomed? Am I at dire risk of magnifying a childhood preoccupation with one parent's gloom while completely absolving the non-depressive one? Do I hold you responsible for the roads I had to walk, the injuries I had to nurse?

Things happened to me that I cannot tell you about. If I could not find the words when I was eleven, it is understandable, but even now I don't have a deep enough vocabulary.

(Tell him, tell them, my sister would encourage. Our

parents need to know what happened to you. They let it happen to you.

Why? What will the telling do? I lost my childhood, irrevocably, so long ago, and the only place it now exists is in their heads. Let it be …)

Talking, not listening, was your forte. The words, like the thoughts, had looped for years, no way out.

You said you wanted out, and I believed you. What you meant was that you could not continue as you had for so many years – emotional, impractical, temperamental – and you were too frightened to change, to go back to the drawing board. The uncertainty of daily living, its haphazardness, had made a lonely man of you. Only two remedies had seemed potent – intoxicant and death – and how easily the two fused for you.

Reminding me of that is this green diary, the one found below your pillow, the pillow we burnt after you left for the morgue.

The shake in your hand that we saw for the last three years of your life is now a shake in the lettering on its page. Read me aloud, it says, and then, don't.

A diary belonging to the year 2001 used by a man dying in 2014 – surely you will appreciate the irony of writing into the past. You use it like a notebook, unmindful of the dates, but they are there, staring at me. Did they also stare at you when you wrote?

Did you also notice that 1 January happened to be a Monday in 2001? A symmetry you would have liked.

My eye traces your familiar hand on the page. You have numbered each of the sayings and proverbs that fill the opening pages, some translated from English, all of them in the Kannada script.

633, that's how many you have numbered in the first set. From the pages marked January all the way to March.

Some of these quotes have been ticked, marked, set aside, and it makes me want to pick those out.

No. 395 – good deeds done for praise are futile

No. 167 – the greatest education is to facilitate livelihood

No. 97 – history is a tomb built on the grave of dead events

No. 58 – if life is to be joyous, our speech and our actions have to be simplified

No. 306 – deeds done with a good mind are like prayers offered to god

No. 181 – sports does not always provide pleasure, but there is no joy without sportsmanship

No. 312 – giving birth and raising children is not enough, giving them education is also duty

Folded in the diary I find a letter, addressed to

nobody and signed 'true friend', promising to always be there 'come what may'. And it has been written by you – who did you mean to send it to?

April is empty. So is May. But July is full of more numbered wisdom. This time nothing is marked as important. There are 194 quotations. All the way into the second day of August.

August, September, silence again. But on 1 October, the words resume just for five more days – more poetry this time, mostly couplets, extracts. And the alphabets are trembling more than before.

The rest of October and November is very quiet, just empty spaces.

It is December that starts to break my heart.

The lettering is harder to read. More quotations. A few pages of silences. And then comes 15 December.

I see poems in Kannada that you are careful to attribute to yourself. These are no borrowed sayings, this is your voice and you want to make sure the diary knows it.

This is the first. I translate roughly in my head as I read:

Birth is accidental, death inevitable
Between birth and death, a life of worry
And yet this desire to live, till the end.

Enough. I cannot, I should not translate you. This language, this poet-father are like distant waves – hypnotic but distant. Let the rest be just between you and me.

My eyes turn to the one under 18 December. It's a poem called 'Me!'. It talks about being a drunk, which you declare is far less of a crime than being a hypocrite. Your attention, you say, is only for those who truly love you, and your obeisance is only for those who act as they speak.

You are not much of a poet. But your voice floats across eons. It smells of earth. Till the end you believed it was a greater joy to give than to receive.

What have I received? What have you given me?

This green diary on my table, is it you?

From 15 December to 22 December, you compose, and then lapse into another patchwork tapestry of words collected and copied with care. Like a Baya weaver bird, you forage for the perfect twig, the loveliest blade of grass, the resilient straw, all words belonging to others. And somewhere in there, you have nested, you have enclosed your own words to yourself.

And I remain an eavesdropper to the dead.

I now see that there were no beginnings in the narrative that had been sold to you as life, only fragments, and only ends, only ends.

It is all over. You are gone. Like the lights.

When the lights went off, you would drag out your bongo drums (how you loved drumming!) and we would sing those old mournful Hindi film songs, you and me in perfect unison, singing into the dark for hours and hours—

I was like the canned laughter for your jokes, the straining ears for your stories, the devoted spectator, and what we shared in my infancy was raw and honest, just between you and me—

The smell of your collar, the lilt of your lullaby, the metal chain of your watch cool against my skin as you rock me to sleep – the memory of your love is older than the memory of your pain, and all that remains now is memory—

The way you gave us a bath, scrubbing our little arms and soaping our hair, as though we were buffaloes in a village stream—

The way you cut out elaborate lace patterns from a paper folded eight ways—

The way we walked together, same gait, same pace, long stride after long stride—

The way you sat us down on a newspaper and gave us nifty haircuts with the kitchen scissors—

The way you wrapped and sealed any parcel in a precise meditative way—

The way you recited long-worded poems entirely from memory, every word a jewel to you—

The way you taught us to cut vegetables, finely, evenly, the knife like an extended finger—

The way you collected and displayed little Ganesha idols, especially those from each place I visited, your faith and my travels tied together—

The way you wrote my name with large loops in all my books—

The way your entire being brimmed to the plaintive singing of Mukesh, each song sadder than the other: *Khush raho har khushi hai tumhare liye*—

The way you hovered around your old red typewriter and me, teaching each finger to find its alphabets—

The way you stood at train and bus stations in different cities, your eyes filling up, your teeth biting your lips, when the wheels started to turn, taking me away from you—

The way you watered your plants with watchful trickles of water—

The way you cried all the way home, for more than three hours, when you saw how close I was to giving up—

The way you could add lies to a true story and still keep it true—

The way you were always you, so flawed, so unbearably flawed—

You, my father.

Leap

(one-act play)

CHARACTERS

W – a woman in her early forties. She wears long flowing clothes in muted earth tones and is barefoot.

M – a man in his mid-sixties. He wears a slightly oversized t-shirt, preferably in bright colours, and aged trousers.

S – a shadow, a woman of no specific age wearing all black, including black shoes, socks and gloves. Her face is painted black. S represents different possibilities through the play – an individualized quirky character, a voice in the woman's head, the dark illness itself, an echo of the dramatic tensions between the other two characters – and is meant to be played in all these shades. Hence it is important to pay attention to shifts in tone.

SCENE ONE

One half of the stage is cluttered with low stools and tall piles of books placed between them. The other side is an elevated platform with a sturdy ladder propped against it. The platform should be broad enough to accommodate two characters and a few strides, and the ladder should be between the audience and the platform.

Two spotlights fall at a distance from each other among the books. The platform is poorly lit but reveals S sitting on it with dangling feet. A streak of light slants diagonally near her.

S holds out an open book so the light beam falls on it and starts to read loudly.

S: I wake to sleep, and take my waking slow.
I feel my fate in what I cannot fear.
I learn by going where I have to go.

W has walked into the other half of the stage and is standing in the dark listening intently.

S: We think by feeling. What is there to know?
I hear my being dance from ear to ear.
I wake to sleep, and take my waking slow.

W walks into a spotlight and sits down on a stool. She picks up a book and starts reading very softly.

W: Of those so close beside me, which are you?
God bless the Ground! I shall walk softly there,
And learn by going where I have to go.

Light takes the Tree; but who can tell us how?
The lowly worm climbs up a winding stair;
I wake to sleep, and take my waking slow.

As she is reading, S starts to climb down the ladder slowly. W looks up and then down again. She is pretending to read the book but is watching from the corner of her eye. When S is a rung away from the stage floor, she hesitates, one foot suspended in space. And then quickly scampers up to the top of the platform again.

W and S (speaking together, though S's voice is soft and halting in comparison to W): I wake to sleep, and take my waking slow.

S: I wrote that.

W puts her book down and turns in the direction of S.

W: Theodore Roethke wrote it. Look.

S: I could have written it.

W (*slightly annoyed*): Why are you hovering up there?

S: I am a shadow. I can be wherever I wish to be.

W: You can be wherever there is light.

S: Well, I am here … I have always lived here. Even when the lights go out in the night …

W: You live here, in the library? Is that allowed?

S: Why not? One never runs out of reading material here, and there is so much to read. Books, books, books.

There is a long pause as if both of them are waiting for the other to speak. S holds out the book in the beam of light and then dramatically lets go. W jumps at the thud.

S: And then there's writing, I have many deadlines to meet.

W is walking slowly to the ladder. The spotlight follows her.

W (*in a disbelieving tone*): A free-floating shadow with a writing career!

S: You judge too quickly …

W: My father wrote too. Letters to editors, short articles, a big green diary, but …

S jumps up on the platform, agitated, and starts to walk back and forth.

S: But?

W: I can't tell you more.

S: Writing is okay, but living in the library is no fun. Books make terrible beds.

W: Where did you come from? You must have a home, go home … (*now standing beside the ladder, resting a hand on it*)

S: How does it matter? I woke up one day to find I had become a shadow, and I was living here.

W is now examining the ladder. She slowly climbs the first rung.

W: And what were you before you turned into a shadow?

S (*stops pacing and stands very still*): Why do you ask?

W (*continuing to climb slowly*): I mean, what did you do for a living?

S: I hardly made a living. But I worked very hard.

W: Worked at what? (*still climbing and now midway up the ladder; she lets go of one hand and swings playfully*)

S: I wrote. I went to the library every morning, sat there till the sun went down, writing all the time. Then I came home, boiled some soup, but drank vodka instead and wrote some more … till the end. I wrote even after the end, I wrote …

W (*tentatively*): Are you telling me that you died?

S: Did I? I must have …

W (*starts to climb again*): How many books did you write?

S: Just one, the story of my life. All I knew and imagined and dreamed went into it – a story I kept writing and rewriting. All the things that happened, they faded as soon as I wrote them. And the make-believe stuff started to come true.

W: Then help me write about my father. Write it as he would write it. And maybe it will shape into a life he hoped for.

S: If he is dead, let him be …

> *W has now reached the top of the platform. She reaches out a hand towards S who does not take it and resolutely turns away. W pauses before withdrawing her outstretched hand and climbs up on the platform. They are now standing back to back, looking out in opposite directions.*

W: Do we write as we remember, or do we remember as we write?

S: We don't remember at all. We bead together words,

call it a memory. Writers are such cheats. Ask your father.

W: I hated it when he spoke my life – how can I do the same to him? But you can write about me, and I will tell you about him …

S: I don't recommend it. Your life is small, and there is the sea of unknown around it, full of perils. Anything you say can spear someone's heart, be refuted, denied, damned. You think you are telling the truth, but the truth is a parody. You can never get it right, and I have learnt to forge ahead, to get it wrong. Wrong, but in the right tenor, like crossing between lives. Believe me, being dead is not as complicated as people make it out to be.

W: So, what is it like? I mean, being dead.

S: Absolutely wonderful! I feel neither hunger nor sleep nor desire nor pain … (*voice trails off in sorrow*)

W: How did you die?

S: How else? With a leap.

> *Brief silence. W slowly starts walking straight ahead to the edge of the platform. S continues to face in the other direction.*

S: Why are you not asking me?

W: Huh?

S: You did not ask me why I did it …

W: Every storyteller has to leap, at some time. I would do it too. Write a leap for me too.

S: I'm sorry. You have to make your own story. If you can't … something must be missing …

W: I have known the pains of growing up, kept the secrets a girl learns to keep, fought to be noticed and played to win. But love …

S: Giving is more important than taking. If you want something, say no.

W: You sound like my father.

S: And my father.

W: Nothing happened as I had hoped. I promised him the world, and then meandered away …

S: I remember …

W: I messed up. He deserves another chance. He had so much to say …

S: I remember …

W: I want to forget, start afresh. He will tell his own

story again. And again, I will listen … or maybe I am destined to go, just like him …

She is now standing at the very edge of the platform. S swirls around and the stage is suddenly blacked out.

S (*speaks in the dark*): Wait! Please. Don't do it! … Please stay where you are. It never ends with a leap, it gets worse. Let me tell you more – about the restlessness, the fear, the anxiety, the discontent … Wait, give me a chance to explain it all over again. Let me put you in a story, a story about love and choices. Let me make this all better for you. Let me tell you how it really ends.

Silence.

SCENE TWO

The stage is dimly lit. There are some chairs and two side tables placed haphazardly. The platform and ladder stay in place. On the opposite side of the stage is a study table with an open laptop that is turned on.

W is moving around the stage, rearranging chairs. She is humming to herself. She fusses over one chair for a few seconds, moves it around and steps back.

W: Ready! Lights! (*the whole stage is lit, and there is extra brightness on the chair she has adjusted, like a spotlight*) Enter!

She is waiting expectantly and looking towards the stage wing but nothing happens.

W (*shouts again, louder*): Enter!

M walks out, smiles widely at her and the audience.

M: It feels so good to be out here on stage again. So good.

W (*handing him a sheaf of papers from the table, which he does not take*): Just because it is a rehearsal doesn't mean you take it easy. You are the one who wanted to do this, remember? (*looking at the papers*) Okay, let's start from Scene Two. Your lines first …

M sits down and starts to talk. W sits down as well, to listen. It is not clear if the lines are from the pages or his own. He speaks theatrically and at the audience.

M: I used to be in the dramatics club of our college, you know. I was cast as the heroine in every play. Long slender limbs, hairless chest, narrow hips, large expressive eyes – I made a beautiful woman, they said. And for days they talked about the clothes I wore – a short skirt, a brocade sari, chiffon dupattas…

W: You are an old man now.

M (*as if realizing it just then*): An old man …

W: I did not mean it like that. You have told me about the college days a million times, and we have so much work to do here.

M: I don't like this role. (*waves the pages*) It is about a father and a daughter – he is a retired bank manager, he drinks, and he is unreasonable. Any fool can tell what is going to happen in the next act – he is going to die! It sounds just like us and it is completely unsympathetic to the father.

W: Not everything is predictable. You know he is going to die, but you don't know when or how …

M: Do you know?

W (*first with some annoyance, and then with sadness*): Yes. He will be sixty-six years and three months old. It will be in the middle of a muggy April night. He will be lying across the laps of his friends, on the back seat of a car, as the blood starts to rise up his gullet …

M stands up abruptly.

M (*softly, as if speaking to himself*): So soon …

W: And he was not bedridden, not even for a day. It was exactly like he wanted.

M: Exactly like I wanted …

He gets up and starts to walk away. Turns around to ask one important question.

M: Was I … did this character feel afraid to die?

W (*nods and says softly*): Yes …

M slowly walks away but stops at the edge of the stage. She watches him go.

W: Lights out!

Lights go out, but there is enough light to see the two figures.

M: What happens afterwards?

W: Before matters more than after …

M: You are avoiding my question.

W: I don't know. I haven't written it yet.

Silence.

W: I am sorry to be putting you on stage like this. But you have always loved the limelight. You love to be admired. You love to be pitied. You need the lights to be yourself. Like a sunflower under a travelling sun.

M: Sunsets are a punishment. It is after the sun goes down that the evening turns lonely, very lonely. I would freeze to death if it were not for the lights. The lights – can you please turn back the lights?

W: A little girl watched you slip into the dark, into the cold. You shivered, literally, your teeth clattered, curled up on the sofa, knees folded towards your chest – you were sinking and all she could do was watch.

M: The lights please …

W: That was years and years ago, and yet … yes, yes, lights!

A dim spotlight comes on at the top of the platform. M hurries to the ladder, starts to climb. When he reaches the top, he sits down in the spotlight, rubs his arms as if to warm himself and watches W.

Meanwhile, W has turned on a table lamp (her area of the stage is lit up as the lamp comes on).

M: This is perfect! A great view! I get to watch you, like I have watched you since the day you were born.

W: Fine, watch, but stay quiet and don't jump …

M: Why would I jump?

W: It is the sort of thought that comes to a person at an elevation.

M (*cautiously*): Is it a thought that has come to you?

W (*annoyed*): How can I write if you keep chattering like this!

She sits down at a computer, types for a little while, and then stops as if in the middle of a thought. She never looks at M when she talks – it is either an aside to herself or spoken into the void.

W: There was a time I thought it would be the smart thing to do, a quick way to go. We lived in a high-rise – the walls were unendurable and the space outside the balcony was inviting. Flight. But it did not seem right that the children in the building got to see a splattered woman on the sidewalk … Maybe it would work better, I thought, if one were to swallow all those medicines in the drawer, all at once …

M: What are you saying? (*agitated*) Wasn't it enough that I have obsessed over dying … so that nobody I love has to do it … I have obsessed for all of us …

W: Your method took years and years, decades really …

M: What other way is there? Why are you talking like this? I can bear anything, but I cannot bear that your life should look like mine …

W is silent.

M: Have pity on me … tell me more, tell me all …

W: I never told you what happened. I never found the words. It was summer and I was at this river island, researching for a novel I was writing. I found myself on top of a bridge, looking down at the swirling depths of the Kaveri. The river was brimming with my sorrows. And more than anything else in the world, I wanted to jump, to end it all …

M (*wistfully, longingly*): Oh, to end it all …

W: I knew then that I needed help. I went home, the darkness like a lump of lead in my stomach, heavy, growing heavier, swallowing me up. I did not want to see a psychiatrist, but there was no choice, and he sent me to the psychologist, and I did not want to go there either. It took me a long while to know I was ill, and then it took me a long while to want to get well. All the shadows closed in, all at the same time …

M: Somehow we have to bear our burdens …

W: It was unbearable, this rising tide of despair and hopelessness. I could not forgive myself, I could not forgive him.

M (*looking visibly distressed*): Nobody told us anything. We called your house, we spoke to your husband – he said you had gone to your sister's house. But we knew something was wrong. An astrologer told us this was your darkest time.

W: It was my darkest time. But what was the use of telling you? You lived in your own darkness. You never came to see me. I was dying.

M: I too was dying.

W: I could not breathe. Inky, viscous, it started here (*placing her hand on her stomach*) like a deep, bottomless hole, a well of black water that kept boiling over, over and over. (*Her hand moves slowly up from her stomach, to her chest, her neck, her mouth; then just above her nose, it stops*) I could not breathe.

M: I have lived like that for years.

W: I have seen you live like that for years. How did you do it? How could you help me?

M: I came to see you at your sister's house. It was terrifying. Your hair, your beautiful long hair, was gone, your neck was in a brace, you did not smile, you had shrunk, your collarbones jutted out from your t-shirt, when you looked at me your eyes were empty and unlit.

W: You were shocked …

M: I was shocked …

W: I could not share what was between husband, wife and a festering relationship. That day you did not want to talk about my suffering, only about the possibilities of patching up, of a future that could work out differently. The astrologer had told you that somehow I had to make it work till the month of March, just six more months, then everything would be okay. You pleaded – go, go back to your husband, all will be well if you go …

M: You looked at me as though I was a stranger, you said –

W: If I go I am not going to make it to March. You will lose a daughter …

He buries his head in his palms and stays that way for a while. Slowly the lights go off on him.

W: You could not say much else to me that day. You left by the evening train. Later, Amma told me you reached home and sobbed your heart out. She said she had never seen you cry like that.

Silence

W: You did not ask me to come home. You thought this would make me go back to the husband I had run away from. No money, no roof, I started again from scratch.

I packed my bags and went to live somewhere in the Himalayan foothills. I felt like an orphan.

Silence. She tries to look for him but it is dark on the platform.

W: But all this was a long time ago. It took years but I found a way out of that tunnel, towards health, towards love.

M: I was overjoyed when you decided to try marriage again.

W: But you … why did you never try to believe again?

M: Maybe I did and maybe you did not want to see it.

W: You kept pointing me to the lit end of the tunnel, the circle of light, but you turned around and walked into the other end, the cavernous unlit hole. You never emerged. (*pause*) Hello? Hello? Are you still there? I can't do this play by myself, you know. Hello?

She gets up and paces. Goes over to the table, shuffles through the papers there, picks out a sheet and speaks aloud, like a soliloquy, no longer addressing M.

You see, people die in many different ways. They can die slowly, the life draining out of them, one trickle at a time. They can thunder – 'rage, rage against the dying of the light' – and exit to echoing applause. They might have a moment of peace, a gentle stopping of a heart that is fatigued by years of labour. Some get to make their deathbed speech. A few are ready to go but are rigged up by hospital machines, cajoled, jolted, suspended in almost-life or almost-death. People may starve to death, or be felled by an evil hand or a sudden accident. When you die of old age, all the organs of the body slowly start to shut down, like a theatre after the last performance. In the slowest of deaths, every gasp is counted, every flicker of the eyelid. Or there is the dying that comes with a body ripened with terminal illness, unyielding to medicine, unresponsive to will. Death itself is stillness, lost breath, a flat line. Death matters less than dying. You see, people die in many different ways.

I was thirty-one and absolutely certain that I would not live to be thirty-two. The road had taken too many wrong turns. Hardly had one trauma healed when another burst forth. I could not bear to look in the mirror, I could not bear to be in my own skin. It seemed acutely immoral to take up any more space in the world, consume even one more ounce of oxygen. After months of feeling completely flawed and helpless, this decision to end life felt like the one perfect moment of control. Perfect calm came with perfect certainty. It was time to go.

Lights fade out.

SCENE THREE

All three characters are on stage. M and W are sitting on two stools placed at a distance of a few feet from one another, each in a pool of light. S is sitting on the platform, dangling her feet. She wears a black hat pulled low over her head. She is not lit but a spotlight falls on a pile of books very close to her that she is rearranging.

In the foreground are two black curtains to cover each half of the stage; both are now pulled back.

W (*writing in a notebook on her lap as she speaks*): Loneliness. A woman's loneliness. Managing relationships, managing a family, managing a career, managing life … and in the centre of all this managing is a loneliness that cannot be managed. A loneliness that never goes away. How does one begin to explain it?

M and S talk rapidly, nearly overlapping each other's words. W continues to write.

S: It's your imagination. You think too much.

M: A man feels lonely too. It's nothing.

S: It's nothing.

M: It's your imagination.

S: Go out.

M: Make more friends. Take up a job. Forget the past. You are going to make me proud, I know it.

S: Just relax.

M: Try not to think too much.

S: Trust me. I know all your secrets …

W drops her books and pen, gets up and quickly walks across the stage.

M: It must be my fault. I taught you to succeed. I goaded you. But when things went wrong … I did not teach you to fail. How could I? I did not know what to do with failure myself. We should learn from others, those who make the formula look so simple – get a job, get married, have children, build homes, retire, grow old, die.

W closes the curtain on S's side of the stage as M is talking. She comes back to her seat and looks at the audience instead of M when she talks, but his eyes are always on her.

W: How can you say that? Life is also poetry, music, art, a monsoon cloud, a bird on my windowsill …

M: Did I teach you that?

W: You taught me to live like a glass bowl – completely

transparent, always willing to accommodate others, fragile in thoughtless hands.

M: When you left home, I was certain you would find your way. When you found a mate, I was certain he was worthy of you. When you drifted, I thought that was what all gifted individuals do. You drifted …

W: I was a kite, precocious, but I did not know the power of the wind, I did not know clouds are just vapours …

She stands, mimicking the release of a kite above her head and M gently holds out his hands as if he were holding the string.

M: But you took flight …

W: Yes, a kite that was free to float away in the blue…

M: And mine was the sorrow of the earth losing to the sky … (*a brief silence as they both watch the same imaginary kite fly*) I could not track the wind currents or your flight. You tugged and the string was cutting into my fingers. I let go … (*his hands drop suddenly*)

W (*slumping back on her stool*): In truth, I was not flying but drowning. There is this thing – this shadow – and deep nightfall in my head … drowning, drowning …

M: What shadow? Is it me?

W: It sounds like my own voice but it feels like you. This sadness you have felt for years, I have known it too. Even if you go, even if I stay well, there will be others like us.

M: Nobody will understand.

W: It is too late. The story is being told and there are listeners out there.

W gets up and while M talks she draws open the curtain covering the ladder. S is now sitting on a middle rung of the ladder. The spotlight is on S, head bent low, a black lumpy shape. W returns to her stool.

M (*talking as W is moving the curtains; now looking at her pleadingly*): We are different, you and I, we are alike. We want to do our best, we want to believe the best in everyone. Let's keep it like that. They will never look at us the same way again.

W: So many people you have helped. So many acts of generosity without any expectations. So much outpourings of love. Where was everyone when you started to crack, when you shattered?

M: Hush. It was our lot to endure.

W: It is not too much to ask – to ask for empathy …

M: Hush. You are asking for the world! They will think you weak. Why plead?

W: It is the strong people who struggle, who pay a price for pushing against the current – the depressed are not weak-minded.

M: I am NOT depressed.

W: How can I convince anyone if *you* continue to deny it? Maybe it starts with accepting the illness.

M: No. And you are wrong to accept it for me. What comes next?

W: We need to see a doctor. You need help with this.

M: No.

W: Yes.

M: No.

W: I am sorry for forcing a word on you that is mine, that belongs to modern medicine but not to your life. What chance do we stand if we do not speak together? It will go unsaid …

M: Always so stubborn! Why humiliate me like this? I fought and resisted any kind of disappointment, and there was an avalanche of those. Sure, I intoxicated myself to cope, but that is not illness. All I have at the end of a long struggle is an idea of my own courage and fortitude. Don't take that away from me!

W: I am sorry, I have to do this.

M: Why hurt the family? Why not let it go?

W: Because. The hurt has already happened and the sharing is a possibility of healing. Sometimes I too wish to forget, so that it never has to be said. If one stirs and cooks it long enough, it will evaporate, disappear. That has been the hope all these years, but it only condenses, sticks to the bottom of the pot, rots there. Silence will seal its fate.

M: Talking has been my undoing. Writing is yours. It is a good thing you have no children. I wish I had none!

W gets up with a start, turns away, her head bent with the weight of silence and thought. At this S scampers down to the floor of the stage.

W (*standing between M and S*): What if this is a loneliness not caused by anyone but myself? What if this is a loneliness that never goes away?

As S and M talk, W walks over to the curtain on M's side of the stage.

S: It will never go away.

M: Talk some sense into yourself.

S: Talk some sense into him.

M: Be optimistic.

S: Be courageous.

M: Be reasonable.

S: Be mine!

M: All this – they are just words.

S: If there are no words, what will your soul live on?

M: You can never trust a writer.

S: You can never trust the dying.

M: Stop now, before you write too much. This is one regret you will not be able to undo. Listen to me.

W resolutely draws close the curtains on M's side of the stage. She then walks across the stage towards S who quickly climbs up to the platform. W sits down on the bottom rung of the ladder, in the spotlight, facing the audience.

W: I could barely survive three years of the illness. How did he manage for decades?

S: Forget him. He needed the disappointment as much as his idealism. Can't you see? He has wallowed in his misery to his heart's content. Nobody else mattered. His family was supposed to suffer with him and for him. He certainly succeeded in that.

W: You are the worst type of cynic. You have no life to look forward to. Don't you feel lonely here? Don't you wish—

S (*cutting her short*): It is childish to make wishes. Not everything has to be about you or me.

W (*standing up as if struck by a thought*): He is right. All this talking is in vain. Nobody is listening. The more I give it a name, I humiliate him, I expose myself.

S: The more tormented a writer, the greater is the clarity in the writing.

W (*puts her head in her hands and shakes it in despair*): Shut up! Don't you ever stop? I need to think …

S quickly lies down. She drops her hands as if to touch W's head but does not. S's hand caresses the air above W's head. Her voice is gentler.

S: You said it would end at thirty-one. What happened? Why did you change your mind?

W: I did not change my mind. That old self did die – that old life sweated, bled, oozed its way out of me.

S: Your choices were limited, but clear. You can go on for years like that man there, pretending the illness is the cure, till one lone organ, the liver, spoke the truth of death. Or you can leave with great conviction, just like I did, with one leap.

W: I was taking all these medicines – they were supposed to help me sleep, supposed to make me less sad, and there were all these other medicines for every real and imagined ailment. I had always joked about the pharmacy in our drawer, and the joke was both handy and deadly serious now. (*She begins to enact her words*) I filled a bowl to the brim with all the medicines I could find, especially the ones that would put me to sleep. I poured out a glass of something, I don't remember, but it came from the liquor cabinet. I typed out a farewell email to someone in another country. I apologized to the dog for leaving under her watch. I was ready …

M: The dog …

Both S and W turn their heads to look at the same spot on the floor.

W: The dog would not take her eyes off me. She knew I was ready to go. She had watched over me for days, weeks now, doing all she could to keep me in this world. That night, she knew she would have to try her hardest. (*mimics the action of pushing a dog down, a dog that is jumping at her arm, pushing her back*) Stop it, stop jumping – what's wrong with you?! Leave me alone – stop it!

S: I saw it too. She had never jumped at you like that before, her paws pushing into your arms, again and again …

W: I did not have the heart to lock her away, I did not have the heart to let her watch me go – we just wrestled on, the two of us, woman and beast, for long … how long?

S: Till … the doorbell rang.

They both turn their heads as a doorbell rings. Neither of them moves. The doorbell rings again. W gets up with a start.

S: You and I were sharing heartbeats that night. I begged you not to open the door. I was ready to leave, so were you, but then … why did you stay behind?

As S is talking, W is pulling the curtains close on S's side.

S: Tell the truth, even if painful, it is redemptive. And it is the greatest offering of love you can give him.

(*realizes that W will be pulling the curtain over her and raises voice*) Wait, don't shut me out. I am wrong, this is not about him, this is about you and me. Listen to me. Listen. (*doorbell rings again, more urgently*) Answer the door. You will live to write about it. And the story reads better this way. Don't you see it? A telling has more depth than silences. Wait, don't do anything in a hurry. Let me read you the rest of the poem –

As S begins to recite the last stanzas of the Roethke poem, W hurries over to open the curtains on the other side, where M had been seated. The stage is lit and empty. She runs down the stage and looks around for M but he is not to be seen.

S: Great Nature has another thing to do
To you and me; so take the lively air,
And, lovely, learn by going where to go.

This shaking keeps me steady. I should know.
What falls away is always. And is near.
I wake to sleep, and take my waking slow.
I learn by going where I have to go.

As the last lines of the poem are being read, W runs over to S's side of the platform and hastily pulls open the curtain. It is empty too. She clambers up the ladder and walks around the platform, looking for them both.

Suddenly she stops still on the same edge that had tempted her at the end of the first scene. She turns and looks at the audience.

The stage is engulfed in darkness.

One More Reason Why

SGM, my father, was born an old soul. Like me.

He had a father who was prone to mood swings and explosions of rage, a father who left a deep imprint on him. Like mine.

SGM had a compulsion to retell his life many times. Each time he tinkered with the telling, it was a recasting of his life too. His life was his material and he flaunted it constantly. An audience was never lacking. Wherever he went, he gathered a crowd around him, or he would put a friendly arm around a passer-by and hustle him over for a cup of tea, or it would be groups of friends (for he made friends everywhere) and relatives (he made friends out of some of them) who sat back to be entertained by his tales, or it would be us, the three women in his house who heard of the same event one more time but never exactly the same story because some little detail would be different – if he had to err, it would be on the side of exaggeration, never prudence. At the end of forty years of telling and listening, many details had gone on to become shamelessly distorted, but nobody cared. Nearly every event was something that had happened to him or had been witnessed. Very rarely did these narratives venture far back enough to encircle his childhood.

His childhood was folded inside him, an origami in the making, and would stay folded. Like mine.

Sometimes, a child-self would be mentioned, but in a material sense. It would be about the grandfather who doted on him and gave him big beautiful coins that are now lost. Or about the massive house this grandfather built, with a door so hefty that it would take four people to close it. Then a few references to a father who refused to be photographed, a tough-willed mother who was querulous, an extended family of many children under one roof. Our father was among the older children, or maybe his sphere of awareness was always towards the younger children around him. He thought of himself as a big brother.

My childhood is like a Monet oil painting – all details are there and yet not there. His is a late Turner – one rousing detail, the rest effect.

That detail has to do with his high school. While he was growing up, a child could only study till the seventh grade in the village school, after which one trekked to the nearest town to complete high school. The girls in the family, not allowed to travel, studied only till the seventh grade and the boys continued on the education track to get as far as their brains and means took them. In those days, my father said, one had to choose a stream of study (science, commerce or arts) in the eighth grade, and for a boy dreaming of becoming a doctor, it had to be science. That is what he had thought he would do.

There he is, in his tellings, a young boy invited to have a conversation with his school principal who informs him that the government has given permission to expand their village school into a high school with eight, ninth and tenth grades, and this was possible that very year. The catch was that they needed a minimum number of students to be able to do it, and they were short of one boy. Would he stay back to study in the village? It would mean he would have to study commerce or arts instead of science, for a suitable science teacher was yet to be hired, and it would mean that the doctor dream would have to be postponed or cancelled. But. The little boy would be doing a great act of sacrifice and generosity for the whole village, for his little sisters. What would he choose?

At twelve or thirteen, faced with this possibility of gargantuan selflessness, the boy said, I choose to gift a high school education to all the little girls in the village, to my own younger sisters, and never mind my own doctor dreams.

This is how my father told it, with billowing regret and an expanse of philanthropic pride that would become the leitmotif of his moral world. To be born the elder child is to sacrifice, to give up. He said this to me repeatedly, and this is among my earliest memories of him. It was imperative for him to see me give my sister the first pick of anything or to hand over my things to whoever fancied it. Charity did not begin at home for him – it was his home.

An afternoon comes to mind, from when I was the same age as he was in his high school sacrificial story. We were expecting some acquaintances – a family of adults and children – to drop by. The adults we did not care about, but we feared the nature of those particular children. They were not like us – they were vociferous, self-assured and demanding. The sequence of events was predictable to us even at that age. Objects would be pointed at, such as my favourite doll (the one missing an eye and a hand) or any of the odds and ends we have collected (shells, feathers, stamps), and we would be ordered to hand them over, most likely to never see the beloved object again. How we scampered around, my sister and I, hiding whatever we could hide before the visitors came, and how we heaved a sigh of relief when they left without our meagre worldly possessions. We felt exhausted and triumphant.

The expression 'to give someone the shirt off your back' has made complete sense to me only in the context of our father.

He would give you the shirt off his back, whether you were in need or not, just because you liked it, and even if it meant he had no hope of ever owning another shirt. He would also give you the shirts off his wife and children's backs. And if we had no shirts, he would go around and find you one somehow, even if it meant he had to grow cotton, make yarn, weave cloth and stitch it with his own hands. Such was our father.

Everyone agreed – yes, he would give you the shirt off his back, such a good man, this SGM.

The training started early with us, and it was thorough. We were told to never be brats, to see the path ahead as not acquisitional but one of denial. And Discipline was the main organizing principle of parenting. The rule was to never say 'I want'. If one is asked 'Do you want?' then one should say no, irrespective of desire or need. We were barely two feet tall when we knew that the slightest possibility of getting something we wanted lay in refusal. If perchance we did say yes, we would never get it – for that, my father was sure, was what spoiled children.

The same concern about not spoiling children lay behind the stick, the belt, the slapping hand.

There was no awareness that children might end up feeling utterly undeserving if turned into monks who have to hone an ability to refuse, and that it leads to a murky adulthood of repeatedly saying no when one means yes to friends, lovers, authority figures, one's heart.

My sister G ran away from home once. At barely nine or ten years of age. Her tender spirit broken from the strain of saying no to herself and yes to anything my father decreed. He was absolute in the way one had to live – it was his house, and we did as he said. This applied to my mother too. She cooked, cleaned, took care of the kids and lived by his ways. To adore him, to obey him – her brief was streamlined – and when she did disagree, it was calamitous, but that is the story of their marriage and my bystander's rights only go thus far.

But it is true that G did take flight from home. It was night, the television was raucous in the background, a Delhi smog had settled into the humming streets, our apartment that hovered two flights of stairs above the streets was a nervous hive. Our father was shaking with rage. G had just said no in a rare moment of rebellion. She just could not take it any more, none of us could, I can now see, but we were tightly pleated in his misery and fury.

I am leaving, she announced, and took her school bag and walked out the door.

Why the school bag? No clothes, no toothbrush, just the faded satchel with a few books. She did not care for her books, but she needed luggage – the gravity of the situation merited it – and this was all she had.

If the television was on, he must have been sprawled on the sofa, he must have been drinking. My mother must have been in the kitchen. In my mind's eye, as I revisit that moment, this is always what I see. I am not sure this is how it was. What I do remember distinctly is the little girl in the sort of utter defiance that could have only come from unspeakable despair, walking out of the door, down the steps, two flights, and then darkness.

A door led out into the street. I stood on the balcony, peering below so I could see her emerge from the door. I was terrified she would disappear into the night, that I would lose her. I leaned over till I was at risk of falling down, but there was still no sign of her. Could I have missed her in the shadows? Was she really gone?

I bolted down the flight of stairs. There was nobody at the landing. I pushed the door open, and there on the last few steps that led to the street was a huddled figure, with her school bag, wanting not to be home but with nowhere else to go.

I sat down beside her. She was crying, but very quietly. Maybe I was too. There was just a large, silent, unseen river of tears and we were islands in it. That is all I remember of that night. Eventually we climbed the steps back to our apartment, but first we sat there together on the roadside, the night swinging low over our heads.

~

I did not want you – you often said to your younger child – it was all your mother's doing, I was happy with just one child. In later years, in the throes of your darkness, you wished you had not brought any children to this world. You even wished yourself unborn.

Please come back to life, please go back in time, please love us equally, please love us kindly. Your love hurt just as much as your anger did. Can we please start this story all over again?

~

I worry about sweeping up your life into tidy explanations and try to stick to your versions about your life, but I am aware that these will be the versions I remember. I could plead that I am a hoarder of memories and the catalogue cards in my head are rarely misarranged or misplaced. But that would not suffice. I look for a pattern, an emergence, trajectories of something you refused to name. In my hand is a magnifying glass, and in my head is a thread, a quest for a shadow that I have known and that had engulfed you.

But to you, melancholy was not a condition, a state of mind or a phase – it spanned your entire life. How can that possibly be explained now in the wake of your death?

You attributed any spell of despair to the incompetence of the world or to specific events or people who disappointed and hurt, but never thought of it as sustained sadness that you could not let go. All decisions were taken in a high emotional tenor. Anything even remotely calculative or measured was distasteful. Everything appealed in its extremes – if you liked someone, you would listen to their every advice, treat them like royalty – and you took your decisions with great flourish and impulse. When things went wrong or caused even the slightest inconvenience, you cursed fate and moped. A little foresight and planning would have yielded far better results, but there could be no planning in your world – the need was to gamble at any cost. You watched the roulette wheel of life events turn, all chips on the table, and no matter where it stopped, the outcome for you never matched the stakes – it was inevitably bad luck.

People around us saw a bank official with a steady income – for you did climb up the clerical ladder slowly, become a branch manager – but there was nothing in your own bank account. I was clearing your books one day when I found your salary slips. Endless loans and monthly deductions showed on the paper, almost nothing left in balance. How did we survive on the paltry amount you got every month?

One hesitates to call it poverty, for it was the kind that came cloaked in dastardly middle-class appearances, so taut that even the smallest unforeseen expenditure could break our spirits. We got to eat each day and our mother constantly struggled to stretch household provisions till the end of the month, but that was it. There was no question of asking for more, objects or outings, and definitely no cash to spend. Clothes were handed down or gifted by relatives, unless it was our birthday, the only time we got to go to the store. You do not know this, but we would wait for the old newspaper pile to grow, so that we could tie it up into bundles, haul them to the market to sell for a few notes, all three of us flush with the pleasure of having spare change that did not need to be accounted for, to buy small pleasures by the roadside. We thought of the better life as being able to own more than two pairs of frayed underwear, not having to wait for one pair to wash and dry in order to change. We saw you turn into hoarders, both you and your wife, storing away every stray piece of wire and cardboard box, and it is easy to see why.

His hands have holes – I have heard this said about you – he is generous, a spendthrift, incapable of saving money.

Your wallet was always open for others. You spent as if you were a king with a bottomless treasury. You splurged on your friends. Any spare cash, after the burst of spending elsewhere, was needed for the daily bottle of rum, for cigarettes, for the paan and tobacco you chewed, and we could not possibly save that money. The smoking only lasted a few years – your wife had bronchitis and we girls were coughing too, so you threw that last cigarette away with a flourish. But there was no time to celebrate, for the drink and chewing tobacco would increase to compensate.

You would die without the intoxicants, you said.

You will die because of them, I repeatedly told you. We were both right.

You started to enjoy your drink when we were living in Goa, when you were in your early thirties. I had just started going to school, and G was a cranky little toddler who clung to our mother and cried for hours for reasons we could not guess. Your responsibilities must have appeared unending – two young daughters, the dreary routine of long hours in paperwork and no outlets for the quirky passions that were so distinct to you. Surely this must be when it first sunk in – a formulaic life stretching out in endless vistas.

Loneliness is never easy to discern with the gregarious ones, although it probably morphs into a camouflaged swamp, just beneath the laughter and talk. You were never without company. And, always at home with children, you never skimped on your love for us – it was demonstrative, effusive, joyous. You laughed, you played, you told us stories.

The happiness of each rising crest seemed to extract from us corresponding ebbs. When you were at your charismatic best, you were unsurpassable, but then the waning, the tempestuous phases would be upon us.

Imperfections of certain kinds niggled at you.

I was ahead of the children in my class in reading and the teacher had not thought my maths needed improving, but I was not particularly good with numbers. You adored numbers, and this was the first sign that I might disappoint, not be the inheritor of your many gifts.

At the kitchen table, you sat with me. I had just been handed a narrow notebook of multiplication tables designed like a telephone diary, with tabs and grooves, handmade with flesh pink and verdant green pages. It was stapled together, my full name on the cover page, and all the numbers written by you with a blue roller pen. I was six or seven, and I knew from the way you gave it to me that night at the kitchen table that it was a labour of pure love, infused with all the hope you had in me. I still have the little book. It is in tatters, and it represents pain.

The delicate pink and green pages fluttered in my little hands, my head swimming from the stack of numbers. My mind refused to absorb or retain the natural beauty and logic of numbers that you always enjoyed. Let me be, let me go, I am only six.

But no, we had to wrestle – such is our destiny. The angrier you became, the more obscure seemed the numbers. Mother hovered nervously around the gas stove, and the young household help in charge of the crying baby sister disappeared into the sole bedroom. You sat in the chair next to me, lit a cigarette, put your hands to your forehead and pulled your hair in frustration. I was supposed to have memorized the tables but it was not working. The pink and green pages started to float in the film of tears clouding my eyes. But the tears could not drop. Nothing infuriated you more than girls who cried. I got it wrong. I got it wrong again. You hit me. The tears dropped. Your anger soared.

I am trying, I am trying my best, but I still don't get it. I look up and the cigarette in your fingers is moving towards me. Smouldering red. You press its glowing tip hard into my skin. Tears cascade, my tongue grapples with the tables again, and fails again. The cigarette descends, again, then again.

~

(My mother knows I am writing about her husband. She sends me a text message, urging me to write about his philanthropic self, the self that he most nurtured and cherished. She reminds me of the charity events he organized, the many blood donations he made, the orphanage and old age home where he volunteered, all the people he reached out to when they were in need.

He wanted to be great, she says, and reminds me to share my father's positive qualities.

I am trying, Amma. I am trying.

And in order to tell one slice of the story, his and mine, with as much integrity as I can muster, I have had to put my mother in parenthesis, much as she has been most of my life.)

~

An astrologer predicted three skirmishes with death for the young man. Whether he would survive or not depended on the antidote, and this happened to be the horoscope of the woman who would soon be his wife. In rapid succession, there occurred three events the family attributed to the prediction – a cobra bit him when he was strolling through a park but a timely anti-venom saved him, he was in a road accident but escaped with a mild injury, and then there was the car crash. The car crash episode was the bedrock of the life-story mansion that my father kept constructing before our eyes. I am tempted to surmise that all his meditations on and longing for death go back to this incident.

The young man, who will later father us, is travelling from one coastal town to another. He could have taken the bus as usual, but he is in a hurry and decides to hop into one of those shared taxis hovering on the edges of the bus stand. Including the driver, there are six people crammed into the car, and the young man sits next to the driver. But a fellow traveller begs him to swap seats and he obliges, moving to the back seat, and off they go on their journey.

The car meets with an accident. Its metal frame is completely mangled (he once claimed he had been slammed all the way back into the trunk of the car, but knowing my father's love of exaggeration that may or may not have happened). A passing acquaintance pulls him out of the debris and rushes him to a hospital. He is alive and there are injuries to remind him of the event. The man who swapped seats with him has been smashed to death.

I think my father turned that scenario around in his head many times. It was a seat he did not want to give up but he did oblige this man, and perhaps in doing so he also gave the other man his death. Is that why he revisited that moment endlessly?

This way of thinking about it helps me understand why this man, who always craved an early demise, wanted to live when doctors informed us that his liver was damaged, that his end could be unpredictably close. The appointment he kept wanting and making with his death was not the same as the actual disintegration. The blood vessels that were bursting in his throat, in his stomach, were nothing like the death that had been fantasized about, and the lure of living was in being able to continue to imagine.

Following that car accident, my father, barely twenty-five years old, would lie to the police and stubbornly refuse to admit he had been in the car. His wounds, he told a suspicious cop, came from a fall. His excuse to us (for the lie) was that he did not want to be summoned to court to give witness. His marriage was just a few weeks away, and he had had a terrible experience with courts and cops the previous time he had been a witness in an accident case, the one that killed a little girl.

There were two bloodied images of my father that literally coloured my imaginings of him in my childhood. The first was him lying in the trunk of a smashed-up car, alive and breathing, so that he could go on to live and have a wife and children.

The second image was of him running through unlit streets holding a bleeding, dying child in his hands, trying to get to the nearest hospital as soon as possible. The child had been hit by a truck that was reversing and the driver had not seen the girl as she darted across the road to run an errand for her father late in the night.

This was something I had to do all the time for my father, so it was easy to think that could have been me. My father was watching when the truck hit the little girl. He picked up the girl and tried to get a ride to the hospital. None of the auto rickshaw drivers wanted to get involved in a 'police case' and soon he was running through the streets with this child bleeding into his shirt, his skin. She would die before he got to the hospital.

He was called to court several times during that trial. The truck driver would beg my father to tell the truth – the child hurried into the unlit street without warning and the driver did not want to go to jail for a mistake he could not avoid. The father of the dead girl would cajole our father to say otherwise – he was miserably poor and needed the compensation money. I don't know how the trial ended, because that part of the story interested our storyteller the least – he was invested in the theatrical and traumatic part (him running through the streets with a dying child) and he wanted to talk about the moral dilemma of bearing witness (to decide to tell the truth was easier than deciding what truth and whose truth).

We were certain we would never have any accident story to match his and listened in awe. Those were the days when we had to walk to school (in Bangalore) – my sister and I, both of us with satchels on our backs and a tomato-red plastic basket in our hands that contained our water bottles and lunch boxes.

There was an iridescence to the morning light that day which colours my remembrance each time, or maybe I have had to recollect this event so many times that the scene has acquired a quality of burnished gold. The ambience has been the only toehold to stay with the episode because the moment of action took place in a twinkling of the eye. A racing bus took a sharp curve at an intersection we had just crossed. The bus was heading straight at us. There were two more children of the neighbourhood with us and instinctively we all moved away from the road. Only my sister was a step behind. Her lunch basket slipped from her grasp and she turned to pick it up. It all took place so quickly, my hand grabbing her and the bus whizzing past us, leaving behind crushed plastic. My sister burst into tears. She had just lost her favourite water bottle – it was shaped like a rocket – and such possessions were rare and truly prized in our world then. It was a rather shaken and sombre group of girls that made their way to school.

One did not look forward to the evening. The demolition of the plastic basket had to be explained to parents. Those days our father flew off the handle at the lightest provocation. Those days I had seen him slap my mother as if she were no different from us. Those days there was a crazed, desperate side to him and we walked around it on tiptoes. First the event was explained to our mother who, like us, worried about telling our father about it. A new basket and lunch box and water bottle would have to be budgeted for and bought. I waited like a convict for a verdict, my nose buried in a book, as she told him what happened.

He called out to me. That familiar way of roaring my name. And then that familiar churning in the stomach as one awaited punishment.

He was holding out his right hand. I was confused. It was not raised to strike. All the fingers pointed at me as if inviting me and I reciprocated with my own hand. He shook it solemnly. I was befuddled, embarrassed.

Thank you, he said.

The lunchbox …

We will get a new one. You saved your sister's life today. I am proud of you.

I do not think of myself as a lifesaver in that story, not then nor now. But his expression of pride at something I did was a significant moment, and it was different from his pride of me as a miniature version of his ideal self.

I wish of course that difference had been clear to me while I was growing up, but it was not.

~

Those years in Bangalore, from fourth grade to seventh grade, are not easy to recollect or write about, even though they contain the happiest nooks of childhood: learning to ride the neighbour's bicycle and then cycling in the sun for hours on rented bicycles, getting a membership card at the local Circulating Library and speed-reading my way through stacks and shelves of books, collecting stamps, learning to whistle, listening to old Hindi film songs on the cassette player with my father, singing on stage for the first time, starting a secret club à la Enid Blyton with the girls next door, watching regular shows on the neighbour's television, discovering I too could write poems and stories. The world was bursting with enticing possibilities.

And yet, mostly, in the cavities of my mind, those years stretch out endlessly, perilously. The bright spots are pushed to the sidelines. Something was going horribly wrong with my little life, and there was nobody I could tell.

I was doing poorly at school – this was around sixth grade – and even though I sat in the front row of my class, my eyes glazed past the teacher, I was unable to pay attention. Daydreaming, said the note from school, but that was not it. Maths felt like carnage, and the marks card, with low numbers inked in red, sat in my satchel, not shown to the parents till the teachers sent word through my sister. Our father thundered, but that had ceased to matter beyond the immediate pain and fear.

My handwriting was the most eloquent witness to those days of turmoil. It changed almost every other day. The pen would sit on the page and not know what direction to take, then turn into grotesque squiggles. As a child who found asylum in words, this would remain the most frightening and shameful experience – all hidden fault lines exposed.

This was also true about standing on the balcony, very late in the night, alone, face turned to the stars. I had started sleepwalking.

In my waking hours, I loitered, hung around the neighbouring houses and tried to delay coming home. One evening I stayed on at a friend's house without notice, as late as I could, and came home to such beatings that for months I felt unable to step out of the room, not even to the toilet, without telling my parents. There had a bright, relatively outgoing child before this, and now there was someone nervous and withdrawn.

One could read these as classic signs and behaviour patterns of an abused child, which was the case, but they went unread.

My father's cousin was staying with us, sleeping in the spare bedroom, an adult man who had a job in a bank. My father and his cousin had grown up in the same house, called each other brothers. I was ten, and quite comfortable sleeping alone on a cot in the living room. One evening – I remember it frame by frame – my father told me to go and sleep in the bedroom with his cousin. He said I would be more comfortable there.

This was a mistake.

The churnings in my father's world at this time were palpable to all of us. His promotions had been delayed. Work was deeply repulsive, unsatisfying, stressful. Underserving peers were getting rewarded and his sincerity was being exploited, he said. He was operating on a short fuse. There were fights about some money that belonged to my mother but had been mismanaged or spent by my father. Their arguments, her deep hurt, his face darker than a mushroom cloud, his way of coping with everything by berating his fate, and when frustration crossed the frontiers of language, by swinging his arms.

That cramping of words – it was my lot too. The

greedy gobbling of books had given me a vocabulary, but nobody had told me about the experience, about what bodies can do to each other. There were no words for this. The predator of my nights was appointed (by my father) as my maths tutor during the day. Numbers became grimmer. I was sent on an overnight bus journey with the man, a sleepless night of such mauling that getting on a bus again felt unthinkable. I could barely function, or I malfunctioned, and that just meant more beatings at home. There was not an inch of stable footing in the cosmos.

In the bedroom, the oil lamps in the prayer alcove lit up the walls late into the night, till the oil or the wick ran out. Then came confusing greyness, odd smells, breathing skin. Inch by inch, night after night, biding time, for the invasion, the pain, the pain.

The words turned up, months later in school, explained by an old nun conducting yet another routine sex education class, while girls giggled into their palms and I sat at the far end by a window, my mouth dry, my heart frozen with terror. It was the most horrifying moment I had known till then. This made babies, I was told, but I had not yet had my first periods, and for the next couple of years, I was haunted by the idea that there was a dead baby stuck inside me. At eleven, the shame and confusion of it all turned my tongue to glue.

(Tell him, tell him what happened to you, my sister would urge me when our father was alive. I had told her in my late twenties, anxious to know if she had to endure something similar. No, she said, to my utmost relief. I also wanted her to know that the innards of my childhood were nothing like its external appearance. But in that moment, what she felt was directed towards our father.

Tell him.

I can't. It would completely shatter him. What purpose will it serve now? He won't believe me, he will say stupid things I don't want to hear. It is the past, it has taken me many years and a lot of work to cope with the trauma. It is best to say nothing, just let it be, let it be …)

I was sutured to my secret. It was soon time for another transfer, for our father's job rarely kept us in a city for more than three or four years. First he was sent to Lucknow, and then to Delhi. But since we were in the middle of school term in Bangalore, he left to live on his own for a year, till we could join him. His cousin moved out of our house too.

With the men gone, the walls of our house seemed to cool down, draw apart. Like saplings cleared to breathe air and light, we sprung back that year, thrived somewhat in the sole care of our mother.

Then something happened to our father in the distant city. We joined him at the end of the year, but whatever he had been resisting had finally claimed him, and the spiral had begun. An icicle of sadness had started to dribble and puddle in me too. This was when G had thought about escaping but never made it past the steps of the building. This was when I turned thirteen, and my father grandly announced that he would not hit me any more, for I was now a teenager. There were a few occasional knocks on the head in the next couple of years, but the days of thumping and whipping were over. We were now hemmed in by rum-soaked evenings.

It was not just the regular drinking, with me, his daughter, made the keeper of the bottles, or the way he recoiled from the demands of parenthood, but the way the anguish radiated from his entire body, sometimes taking the form of intense chills, the dragging feet and bent back that returned very late from work, the surges of anger (one day he emptied my entire writing table out into the streets), the way he bit his lips and groaned that he could not bear it. It is not my place to diagnose a dead man, and back then (I was perhaps in the ninth grade) there was no name for the chronic torment we witnessed. But now I know.

~

(Tell him, tell him …

I can't, I simply can't …)

What mirage was I trying to protect? Even if it shattered you as a father, as a person, even if it served no purpose, even if you did not believe me, even if you said stupid, hurtful things, even if our words clawed at old wounds that I had worked at healing, it did not matter – I wish I had told you.

That adult cousin of yours whose bed I had to share, or the teenage male relative you left me alone with, or the neighbour you trusted to watch over us while we sent kites flying into a faded Delhi sky – I wish I had told you.

You cannot take it, you will erupt, you will drink more, you will cry, rant implode. This was what I believed.

As a man who talked all the time and as a daughter who stored every word in her head, you and I, we were a disaster. You shared your life philosophies endlessly but it was all about an idealistic place. Your entire outlook was predicated on a few keystones – work ethic that demanded selfless hard work, generosity that would rise up to meet any need without any return expected, and above all, faith that people are capable of unalloyed goodness even if the collective was tainted by greed and selfishness. It was particularly the desperate need to trust in the incorruptibility of individuals that caused us trouble.

There is much more we should talk about, if only you could listen outside the lassos of your woes. And perhaps the only way for me to do this now, without condemning you unfairly, is to remember what you would have said to me – the lines not entirely conjecture, for I have heard them from you many times.

I want to say: Your job as a parent was to protect, but you sent me on odd errands late in the evening, unescorted, sometimes with a little sister in tow, in a city roving with predators. Big city, narrow lanes, adult eyes that caged little girls.

You would have said: What could happen? You should be warriors, not cowards. I want my daughters to be like other people's sons – self-reliant, efficient. You will thank me someday.

My future spoke to me in early teenage years, from within the few books you had collected. On a pink tissue-thin paper, carefully folded in half, you had neatly typed out the letter Abraham Lincoln had written to his son's teacher: '*... because only the test of fire makes fine steel. Let him have the courage to be impatient ... let him have the patience to be brave ...*'

I read those lines ever so often, saw your younger self talking to my older self, till the pink paper started to crumble in my hands. The phrase about fine steel never left my head.

I want to say: You have this red motorbike and you drive like the fiend, both of us children clinging to you with our little fingers. A sharp swerve and you keep speeding, but I have fallen off on the street. I am sitting there dazed and have no awareness that my little fingers are not holding on any more. G yells about my fall and you come back for me. I am still sitting on the road. You laugh and turn it into a joke. I look at my bruises and never understand why it is funny.

You would have said: Nothing happened to you. Stop being such a crybaby.

I want to say: No, it has happened too many times. You have insisted on driving while drunk, the two-wheeler wobbling dangerously, and sometimes you have insisted on taking two women as pillion riders. Remember that night when you were drunk out of your mind but would not let us hire an autorickshaw. You screamed at us, insisted we ride with you. Every minute of that crazy ride, completely unsteady and dangerous, I was petrified, certain we were going to crash. We could have been maimed, dead.

You would have said: You exaggerate. Sure, I had a drink, but I was perfectly in control. Didn't I bring you home safe?

I want to say: Sometimes you just forgot I was out in the world waiting for you. I was in high school and you dropped me off for an inter-school competition, an unfamiliar venue, promising to pick me up later, and then did not turn up. I had no phone number, no money, no option but to stand there outside locked gates, beside a road clogged with vehicles, while everyone left, and strangers slowed their vehicles to look at me. On the pavement, in a hostile city, I waited and waited. There was deep relief and regret in your eyes when you saw me that night and you said – I am very sorry, but I forget about family when I am at the office, and I only remembered you when I was locking up.

I want to say: You hated taking medicines or taking us to the doctor. When we had a cough or fever, you would give us some rum to drink, neat, and we would totter to bed, tipsy kittens. Surely there is a law somewhere about doing that to children. Marriage, pregnancy, child care, there were so many times we needed you to be a father, to be sober, but you never missed that drink.

You would have said: I have always lived for other people. Drinking is the only thing I do for myself. I drink with my money and I drink in my house. Don't worry, I won't come and beg you to take care of me when I am dying.

I want to say: You have been in the business of dying for years, and everyone has been suffering it. Do you know how many times you have passed out, and we have had to drag you to bed? Do you know how long you sit at the dinner table, each morsel taking ages to find its way to your mouth? How hard it has been for your wife to put up with it, night after night?

You would have said: Both you girls, always siding with your mother! She is not what you think she is. She is responsible for me ending up this way.

I want to say: And do you remember the time you took me to the seedy underground bar in that town? No woman must have ever stepped in there for the many decades they have been open. I was not a child then, I was well into my thirties but uneasy nonetheless around those strange men. You insisted I drink my coke straight from the bottle, so that they know I am not one of them. I saw you get so drunk that day, as the men around ogled, while my voice skimmed your ears, your eyes clouded. That day I watched you through a shimmer of tears, as you tried to gather imaginary morsels from the table, eating your own dribbling spit, the full plate of food lying untouched an inch away, your head swaying dangerously close to it.

You would have said: Did you consider what I was going through? I was taking care of my dying mother. Did you see the state she was in? Bedridden in her nineties, and I had to clean her urine, her stools, her vomit. Why is she suffering like this? I cannot bear to watch it. It is more than I can stand. I won't be able to do it if I did not drink.

I want to say: Ever since I can remember, you have told me not to have children. You thought it the worst thing one could do – bringing innocent souls into a cesspool of misery. You said it too many times. I could never think of motherhood without your voice in my head. But I loved children, thought I would have my own.

You said: Learn from my experience. And I have seen what marriage and motherhood has done to the women in my family. You are meant for better things, great things.

You often held forth on the virtues of virginity, very difficult for any abused child to hear, and about the dangers of love. The first time I fell in love, you knew it. And it made you sad. I had a talk with you about this, without naming the young man, though you may have suspected – I was always so obvious. You told me to be careful, that love would hurt, and that one had to love anyway.

I want to say: We left home as soon as we could, just as we turned twenty, to study in distant cities. Parents of other students visited, at least once. Not you. Wait, there was this one time. You came on a very short visit, without any advance notice. I was not around when you turned up, and you went away to spend the rest of the day with your friends. They mattered more than me. Later, we talked on the phone, but it was time for you to return, without meeting me. I cried so much that day. You never came again.

You said: I wanted to surprise you. I also had to meet my friends. Don't cry …

I want to say: You have had many good friends, but an equal number were dubious. A girl child without sensible parents is like a fenceless field, open to encroachers. I don't feel safe in the world. I sleep poorly, with great difficulty, just a couple of hours each night.

And that one time, I did say to you: I don't like this friend of yours, the one who behaves differently with me when you are not looking. Eyes of lust, kisses blown in the wind, suggestive winks. He slapped my face for something silly in the presence of my mother.

Already he has started to treat me like his possession. I don't want to have anything to do with him. He is your friend, not mine.

You hit the table instead of me, kept hitting it. You accused me of being disrespectful and rude. Your daughter is like a daughter to your friends too, you claimed.

It would seem that you and I would talk at cross purposes about pretty much any memory I can muster. But for people who know us, we are more aligned than apart. My mother, your wife, has said it to me enough times, and often in a tone of exasperation: You are just like your father!

During the early years of my life, when I idolized you as heroic and infallible, these were words to be cradled against one's chest, to absorb and reflect on with pride. I wanted to be exactly like you.

But that changed during the years you towered over us, wrathful, leather belt or lit cigarette in hand, punishing yourself and us for living in an uncaring world, and then weeping your agony like a child. I looked at you and thought, that cannot possibly be me.

You are just like your father!

These words kept me tossing through long nights. I would sit up while the household slept, my face resting against the grills of an open window, inhaling the vegetal fragrances of the night, and worry about how not to be like my father. I agonized that my mother was right – for aren't mothers supposed to know their children best? – and what on earth would I do walking the earth like this cursed Frankenstein? Could I please be like my maternal grandmother, the sacrificing enduring saint?

You are just like your father!

The first time I knew that was not true, with the deepest certainty, was when the Babri Masjid was dismantled by the swayamsevaks. We watched it in Mysore on our television, those locust-like men descending upon a distant town. I was eighteen years old. You danced in front of the screen as frenzied mobs climbed the dome and chipped away at bronzed beautiful stone. I remember something inside me curdling slowly. You cheered the hooligans – you wished you had been there! You had had your RSS days, when you collected money for the Vivekananda Rock Memorial, when you volunteered to go fish out corpses in a flooded city, when your inherent sense of service could be clothed in the social comfort of Hindu pride and identity. This was your nation, and Muslims were marauders who had no place in it, nor did their mosques, now turning into a cloud of dust on the television screen. It was repulsive to me.

I don't want to be you! It was a liberating moment to know it, and then to say it aloud. I disagreed with your politics much before I could muster the clarity or courage to disagree with your other choices. We argued, and I stood my ground. Dissent or disagreement of any kind needs a language and a tongue to speak that language. I had found both, standing on the edge of my teenage years, as the Babri Masjid crumbled and your eyes watched me with feigned martyrdom.

We did not speak to each other for days following this. There could be no dialogue in worlds torn asunder by violence. I was going to be my own person.

But Amma never stopped thinking or saying how much I am like you, even after your death. How is it possible? I have done much to chisel a different self, to travel away from you, to escape this likeness.

My mother compares father and daughter – self-absorbed and a wild streak that insists on its own reason, generous to ridiculous extents, unattached to money, that same way of trusting strangers and turning them into friends. We work more than our employers expect, never holding back. She remembers there were friends for you at every street corner, and you loved to chat with workers and shopkeepers of all kinds – your geniality knew no hierarchy. There is something of that in me, she says, your way of endearing yourself to any audience. And of course that strong will. Just like your father, she says.

~

Let us match memories, shall we?

The family is inside the cabin of a large truck, the only ride available so late in the night, after a picnic in a remote forest. I can clearly see the motley crowd – father, mother, a toddler, a little girl who looks like me and some distant relative. Inside the truck cabin is one driver, one cleaner and two men who are also impromptu travellers like the family. It is a very crowded cabin, there's hardly any space to stand or sit. Mother gets a seat on priority, her toddler safely asleep in her lap. One of the other travellers, seated on a narrow cushion, offers to hold the little girl in his lap. Father agrees.

The little girl settles in the stranger's lap, facing her father, facing a large pane of glass through which she can see the headlights of the truck on twisted tree trunks that are rapidly moving, the stranger's arms firmly around her. The cabin is dark but for a string of little coloured bulbs above the windshield, blinking around some framed pictures. Nobody moves, only the truck, and then one of the men in the cabin hops off at a town. Father finds a seat, smiles and thanks the stranger for holding his child, asks him to return the little girl to him.

The stranger refuses. His grip around the girl tightens. Father asks again, firmly, but the man refuses. Father asks again, angrily this time, and the stranger refuses with the same finality again. Several times Father asks, and each time the stranger refuses, his arms tightening around the little girl till she has to gasp to breathe. Nobody knows why the stranger refuses. He keeps repeating, she is just like my child. Fine, Father says, but give her back to me.

No.

Father grabs the little girl's arms and yanks while the stranger holds on.

Pulled in two directions, the girl is in pain but is silent, like a ragdoll. She is aware of nothing but her father's fury. It is magnificent. She dare not blink. Father pulls till the girl is released from the stranger's arms. Her memory of that night ends there.

What do you remember?

~

It gave SGM great delight that all of us in the family, including the dog, had names starting with the same alphabet, G. He had decided a name for me even before he knew I was a daughter, even before he was married, and it had a lot to do with a love of the alphabet, the sound of certain consonants when they met certain vowels. He cared for words as much as he cared for numbers, and it was passionate caring.

If one had to choose a single word that our father brandished often, that he identified with the most, it would have to be Failure. When we were little girls, he explained all about the word, talking frankly to us, as though we were adults. I would think, even say aloud at times: No, you are not a failure. You have shaped us, your daughters, and we love you – isn't that achievement?

A few years after that, maybe because his eyes threatened to rain into the rum he swallowed undiluted from the bottle, I would even be so bold as to promise: I will not be a failure. I will succeed. You can live your life through me.

It is hard to explain what exactly that failure might have entailed, for it was surely more complex than amateur psychoanalysis might uncover. Some of it was personal but much of it seemed to be tied to his professional self, to the job he never made peace with.

But then, around the time he turned fifty, the

nationalized banks offered a voluntary retirement package to its employees, and he eagerly took it. He moved with his wife to Mysore, where they had a little house. The house was the only thing, he would claim, where he was lucky – friends had filled the application, the plot was allotted through lottery, the house was built on bulk government contract, all costs paid by bank loans, not a finger lifted by him.

No doubt the house was built poorly, and he complained about the endless repairs it demanded. Still, it was his own roof, and now finally he had a chance to do something for himself, maybe start that business he talked about, a little shop of gift items. Our ancestors were traders, and one layer beneath his unrequited doctor dream were entrepreneurial aspirations. The bank had given him a bulk amount for taking early voluntary retirement. He finally had the time and the means. With this came a new wariness about money, for he knew as well as everyone around him, that cash would invariably vaporize in his hands. All options were deliberated but he could never take the step towards setting up the business. Perhaps he lost his nerve.

SGM was never cut out to be a lone ranger – that was the sad fact. He always needed hangers-on, admirers, sidekicks, assistants, an audience in the office as much as in the neighbourhood. Losing the office space meant this need would have to be fulfilled entirely by social circles. He would leave home in the mornings, sit outside a nearby grocery shop, chat with everyone who stopped by, especially street dogs, and recruited the boy in the laundry shop to play his personal assistant. Soon, this young man had access to his valuables and financial papers, which even his wife did not. The need to trust and be trusted by strangers was almost an addiction with our father. The public's admiration was heady, it was only too evident, but then he would have to return to the reality of his family that had long ceased to be dazzled by his flamboyance.

I am a failure, he would say for the millionth time. He took to drinking more, in the afternoons too, now that he was home all day, all week.

I didn't respond, I couldn't bear to, and I would think: Fine, go ahead, and think you are a failure, does not look like much else from where I stand.

Or maybe I had stopped looking.

I dwell on this now because it helps me muster some compassion, and not just resentment, for why I was always the screen on which his aspirations played out. My college years were the most promising for him – I brought home awards and prizes with assuring regularity. I was at the top of my class, I won the medals and ranks he wanted, and I looked all set to be a media professional, just like he wanted. But while doing my mass communication course, I changed my mind. Living away from him, my own instincts were emerging and they did not want to follow his script. I drifted from job to job, place to place, and he watched anxiously. I was in no mood to comply, to return to his expectations.

He continued to hope. Every astrologer who had been shown my horoscope had promised my parents that the conjunction of Jupiter and Mercury while Venus ascends in the first house of my natal chart was something to celebrate. Their first daughter was born for fame – she would bring much glory to the family name. More than one soothsayer asserted that it would happen through a compulsion to communicate, a proclivity to language, through writing. Even though my father claimed he did not care for astrology, these predictions aligned with his own hopes. He saw me as a successful television journalist who he could watch on screen each night and who would be envied by the world. He imagined me a writer winning hefty international awards, interviewed in every newspaper. He did not care about wealth, not a whit, for what truly mattered was that I be celebrated, and that the warmth of it spread to his bones.

Sometimes he would murmur, in my hearing, maybe her next book will do it. The reference was to a manuscript that had taken me over a decade to write and looked increasingly like it would be shelved. He had not seen a word of it, but he told himself it was good – good enough for some public acclaim. He also said, I wonder if I will be around to see it.

He died before the book was published. I was Siddhartha the Prince gone wrong. No prophecies were coming true in his lifetime.

In his last years, he continued to talk about my faded glories – awards and prizes that I had won decades ago, stray jobs with celebrities, the only recent bragging point being that I had gone abroad to get a doctoral degree on an assistantship. But none of this was anywhere in the league of the meteoric fame that had been promised.

I too might have tried harder or been apologetic, had not I met a man in my early thirties, around the time I broke away from my father's dream. A man who told me I had no rung to clamber to, that I was already accomplished and that he was proud of me. Not having to wander in search of another's notion of success, I felt complete and beautiful. I had been unknotted from the paternal yoke.

But being unknotted is not the same as learning to

catch the wind currents as one migrates with the seasons. Mine was to be a slow expedition.

~

SGM saw himself as morally upright, incorruptible in his work ethic, a wide-chested canal that cuts deep furrows and nourishes flocks. To others he credited fine virtues and the best intentions. What I encountered in the world as I travelled through it was completely different from what his words had painted for me.

When both his daughters wanted to leave home, in the name of higher studies, to distant cities, SGM was keen for us to go. We were in Mysore then and I moved back to Delhi, and four years later my sister went to Chennai. He sent us whatever money he could spare – it was barely enough to get through the month – and unfailingly with it came a little note crammed with bold writing. The scrap of paper expressed his great desire to see us succeed – it urged me to fly in a tone that pleaded a return to him.

I did return to his hearth when I could, but my heart was turned away, and he tried to understand why he had been knocked off the pedestal. Why did I not idolize him any more, like I did when I was a little girl? Why did I look like I had secrets behind my eyes that I did not want him to know? Why was I self-effacing and embarrassed when he wanted me to perform in front of his friends or when he bragged about me to them?

It was because while he was talking about me, I was not me. My twenty-one-year-old self already felt miles away from the nineteen-year-old who had lived under his roof. Stop, stop, stop, I wanted to say, but he was obdurate, a potter grown attached to the clay spinning on the wheel, so close to its desired form.

After every vacation, I returned to the big city, and the big city swallowed me. It did not matter that I had won awards in my small city. All I had was a colonial library on my side – every Victorian novel and Elizabethan sonnet stacked in my brain – but time had stopped in the early twentieth century in the Maharaja's College library, and the creatures of the big city were ahead by decades. The shock of the deficiency was immediate. I was now in a reputed Masters programme, hundreds of miles of independence between me and family, but there was no bridge between a strained upbringing and the crustiness of that social world.

Things began to unspool in my head. The more candid I became, the more dubious I must have seemed to my peers. Did I even have a personality to claim? Angular edges stuck out, the authentic parts felt pretend, the pretend parts seemed more likely to find acceptance. I scrambled to find alternate personas, to be whatever might seem normal or could spin a cocoon of intimacy. Love was both a compulsion and something to escape. I had not yet figured how to ask for and seek the solace of solitude. Those around me stepped away, as one does when a life starts to unspool, and there was nothing to do but accept what that implied. Perhaps they saw the confusion, the mess, which had grown roots in my head.

The only world that had felt complete till then was the one constructed by my father, and even though I had some idea that his thoughts and experiences were like film reels that could not sync voice and picture, I now had to encounter the enormity of what lay ahead of me. I did not have sufficient life tools to deal with any crisis, and the parents at home had none too. My father's best coping mechanism was to moan and long for death.

A vast continent of ice, and a little icepick in my hand.

A relationship happened and fell apart, and it exhumed demonic shadows of childhood nights.

I had to admit that though suppression had proved a dependable coping strategy for years, it had run its last lap. The memories poured out in volcanic waves. At the first threshold of adulthood, a wounded childhood had to be nursed – there was no other way.

~

Someone recommended K who headed an NGO for women in distress, and I first heard her voice over a public telephone that was clutched too tight. Hello? My ears and my tongue did not work together. Please?

Within a minute, K had given me an appointment. Another day. The journey to her office felt longer than it was, every moment leaden, first a bus ride, then a walk down the busy South Delhi market, standing outside her door on the street, the road disappearing under my feet, wishing to flee, but unable to do anything but drag one foot and then another up a steep stairway. In front of K, what appeared catastrophic in my head, a tidal wave, turned into a puddle, for the words were again showing up as feeble, staccato, inadequate. In over a decade, it was the first time I would tell someone what had happened – about the time I started sleepwalking, the time I lost my handwriting, my frontiers breached in more ways than one. Separated from K by a big table, I felt the utter futility of the disclosure. But as the memories dropped, with tears that would not stop no matter how quickly I mopped them, my biological family ceased to be the keepers of my past.

A few meetings later it was suggested that I attend the afternoon group sessions at the NGO. I tried to join in even though I was like a baby tortoise growing a shell, but learning how brittle it turns with each recollection.

She is the only one in the group who is not interested in sharing her stories with the others. She knits, and knits constantly, her eyes on the moving needles at all times. Other women in the circle look at each other, take turns to speak, but she does not look at us, not even when we are sharing brutal stories. She is rounded, her shoulders are aged mountains, her face broad and inscrutable. I have chosen to remember little of those afternoons, almost none of those heart-rending stories, no other faces that I met in that office – only her.

It is finally her turn to speak. Her eyes mostly stay on the needles, but between words there are furtive glances at her audience. The story is told curtly. She was married to a reputed doctor and lived in the US with their children. She found out that her husband was sexually abusing their daughter, then three or four years old. As soon as she found out, she returned to India with her children and filed for divorce and custody. She had a traditional upbringing in a conservative Punjabi family, her marriage was considered a sparkling success, and she had never held a job. Nothing in her life had prepared her to deal with a situation like this, nor did anyone around her fully comprehend what was happening. Some in the family even wondered if she was imagining things and suggested she return to the marriage. Her husband says she is mistaken but she has seen the look in her daughter's eyes and knows the truth. She has to do the right thing by the little girl, but what is the right thing? No matter where she looks, it is an unknown horizon.

Her voice is a monotone, not a shred of emotion. Only once does the veneer crack. And this is at the end of the session. She looks up at me and has only one question. It is the only time she has met someone's gaze that afternoon and the only time her voice changes. This is when I know she paid close attention to my story – her little girl was someday going to be a woman, like me.

After all these years (after what happened, she means), are you *normal*?

~

In three years, all my possessions had migrated with me eleven times – different shelters, different base camps. These were my postgraduate years in Delhi. I was encountering a city that could be ruthless to a young single woman, an outsider, living on minimal resources, easily wounded, trained to be a foot soldier at all costs.

The sessions at the NGO stopped as abruptly as they started. I could not bring myself to go and sit in that circle of women, not after the woman with the knitting had spoken.

The rapid pace of the city and the course, the wide range of experiences that living on one's own meant – all these were very hard to communicate to a family when one had neither a cellphone nor a computer, only a postal service that could just about carry snatches of life, edited summaries, customary assurances.

... I am healthy, enjoying my course, missing all of you ...

One kept difficult things from a father that one knew was anguished about life's difficulties. His idealism (at that time my idealism too) versus the self-preservation that one learnt on the streets – the entanglements, extrications, negotiations, constant and gruelling. I was completely out of my depth, but never told him. What was the point?

But when there was trouble that found its way to the newspapers, I was forced to tell SGM about it. I was sharing a rented house with my classmates, and a harassment episode in the neighbourhood forced us to abandon the house in the middle of the night. The event turned into a police case, taken up by women's rights groups, even raised in Parliament. Some parents, relatives and teachers were of the opinion that it was best not to make an issue of it, to withdraw calmly. Some of the roommates did that.

Idealism or self-preservation? He and I talked on the phone and I followed it up with a detailed letter. What should I do?

I knew he was terrified about a daughter in her early twenties getting into permanently damaging trouble in the big city. It felt as if I was testing him for the first time. And I was. I needed to know if he would stand by the speeches he had made for all the years I had known him – about not putting up with injustice, being fearless about voicing opinion, putting loyalty above self-interest.

Idealism or self-preservation?

He did not miss a beat: Do what your heart tells you is right. Stand with your friends.

I did what felt right then, and I am glad. That was the last time he and I were in complete solidarity about something abstract and concrete at the same time, and his approval would gradually count less than my hunger for adventure and new experiences. The rest of the months in Delhi that followed did not make for easier living, but I felt contiguous with my father. I was aware he had planted and nurtured some qualities in me, and I had not known if they meant anything in real-world situations, whether they would endure, whether I would be able to play that role and still retain my own voice. I knew the answer when I chose my first job after graduation – a four-month assignment as an assistant director in a movie. SGM received a letter from me, not requesting permission, but candidly informing him of a decision I had already taken on my own. For the first time, telling, not asking.

I had some inkling, as did he, that this was the prologue for my life ahead, and his acceptance, or non-acceptance, was going to be my rite of passage. Just like I'd never take any money or help from him after that job, I'd never ask for approval again.

I received a stoic letter wishing me luck. He wanted to show he could stand by my uncertainties, and I wanted to break away, defy his imagination of me. Neither of us could have fathomed what lay ahead, but we had locked gazes. Who would blink first?

He received long letters with updates. There I was, lugging my bags through remote villages of the Himalayas, travelling with strangers, no contact details given; months later, submerged somewhere in the crowds of Mumbai, working on the production team of a Bollywood film; onwards to another city, churning out videos for a daily television show. Some friends came together to register a media house, my name on the dotted line too – a company that struggled, functioned for a while, then shut down for good. I returned to freelance projects but devoted several months to a fledgling novel till it became a full-time obsession. Then a return to academics, research and teaching, an imminent migration across three continents. It had been ten years since my first job. I had learnt from every fork in the road, loved the richness of its curves, but SGM was slowly tiring of the vagaries of a restless child, tiring of hope. Perhaps if it were just about nomadism or a broken marriage, he would have stood by me. But when I landed in the labyrinth of sadness that he had walked most of his adult life, it was more than he could take, it was hard to hold my gaze. He blinked.

~

I sit to write. A million eyes watch. Faces materialize as I type. Some distant aunt, a curious student, a relative by marriage, an acquaintance in this coastal town – almost paralysing, these future readers. And I know why there are such few memoirs being written in this country about the sort of suffering that only families can inflict and endure. The rhetoric of duty, sacrifice and family honour turns ceaselessly like a giant oil press.

On more occasions than I can count, I had said that I would never write a memoir. Life had been eventful, the sort that has to be ingested and distilled in private recesses. But, even though I had been expecting SGM to die exactly as he did, suddenly and ahead of his peers, it was like an unfinished narrative. He was a bright and extraordinary man, and we had shared an illness that had claimed him, while I had survived. No deliberation was needed – the writing tumbled out within a couple of months after his death. But the tears did not tumble, not even a drop. It was as if only writing could tackle the work of grieving.

Then, nearly eight months after SGM died, after having breakfasted with visiting family, I saw many missed calls from my mother on my phone – an unusual occurrence. The whole world went still. Time overturned. My mind slid to that night when the men accompanying my dying father, my dead father, had desperately tried to call me from his mobile phone, several times, but my phone's battery had stayed depleted. Unreachable.

My hands shook as I called my mother, first on her mobile phone, no response, then on the landline, no response. My fingers pressed numbers again and again till she picked up the phone. She was fine, she said apologetically, it was some small matter she needed to talk about, but my heart would not stop quaking.

There was a roar between my ears as I stumbled to the bathroom, locked the door, looked at my face, his face, in the mirror.

Alone, in the bathroom, I finally cried my heart out. I am sorry, it took me eight months to shed tears for you.

I cried for the loss of a talented life, for the loss of a father, for the years he and we would never have.

What choice was there but to write? He was the easiest man to approach but not an easy man to have a conversation with when we disagreed. He could be abrasive, unreasonable, and there was so much I had never told him. Even now I cannot reveal much of my life, especially the details he was not told but deserved to know. Then there are all those adventures I have had as part of my nomadism, something bequeathed by his life patterns, but none of those are relevant to a story about my father. What frames us together in this literary snapshot remains an illness and a love beyond measure, and so there I stand now.

Depression is negative thinking, my mother insists, and one should always 'be positive'. If one believes in God and thinks positive, there can be no depression. She really believes that. Admirable. But not true, I tell her. It is a dreadful affliction. Her husband died of it. She looks unconvinced.

My sister calls me when the film star Deepika Padukone goes on a television chat show to share her experience of depression. It must have been so hard for you, Akka, when you were ill, she says. What new thing has she learnt, I wonder, and watch a recording of the show on YouTube.

My sister turned up at the watch post through my depression storms because of her love for me, maybe even a sense of duty, maybe because the psychic wounds were festering openly, but this particular tenor of acknowledgement is different. Something else has made itself known after the film star spoke – the medical condition is severed clean from its emotional morass, with only its pathology remaining visible.

Why? It is always the first question depression sparks – where did this come from? Not asked from a diagnostic mood, but in avoidance or curiosity or habit. No doubt the wrong question each time. If it is here, if it is in our midst, we need to ask what needs to be done.

Such is the illness that it seems to warrant silent suffering, as much as the silent moving on. If you were supine on a hospital bed, if your limb was in a cast, if you had a large bandage around your head, if you walked around with warts all over your body, you could claim illness, pain, suffering. With depression, all you have is a clinical diagnosis, some pills and a few words to describe the indescribable, all of which evaporate rapidly in the face of 'be positive', 'get exercise', 'be strong', 'move on' and the unspoken urgings to act like it never happened. The appearance of normality becomes crucial. No matter where depression starts, whether in the caverns of relationships or in the crevice of the brain or in the runnels of the heart, the visible signs of the illness are slow to emerge. At first nothing, and then the sort of symptoms that families are happy to attribute to something else, anything else, anything but this.

And identifying it is never easy. A certain corner of the scale becomes the defining criteria: Will you cause bodily harm to self and/or others? Are you curled up in bed all day? Have you lost appetite, sleep, laughter? This means that the ones who are walking around with some semblance of functionality and productivity, even though they are racked by the devastating illness, will take forever to accept that they need help, and even longer to seek it.

What if you had a broken hand or tuberculosis? I ask the young friend slumped in a chair in front of me, the one who begs for anonymity, and no intervention. Would you want to be treated?

Yes.

Then why the hell are we not talking to the whole damn world, to anybody who cares to listen, anybody who can help you with this constant despair that is likely to kill you? – But I cannot say it like that. I try to find other words, the somewhat okay words, the somewhat okay tone.

The biggest hurdle is that the mind that is unwell and needs treatment will do its best to talk you out of it. No other organ in your body is capable of this – the failed kidney will not articulate its denial. But the mind, even when it is rapidly sinking, will convince you at regular intervals that it is actually not so ill and that it is capable of recovery without intervention. The story of long-term depression often swings between these poles – denial and relapse.

Please promise me that nobody will know.

I promise.

This conversation about depression has happened many times and the range of symptoms is staggering – from feeling listless to wanting to harm oneself – and I try to pour my heart out to the students who walk into my office. I want them to know that it can be survived, that the bottomless pit of darkness can be climbed. It is a precarious process – not to seem patronizing, not to seem self-obsessed, not to push for pharmacological solutions, not to canvas the talking cure, not to do too much, not to do too little.

When one has been somewhere in the vicinity of deep despair, one learns to spy its shape in others, like inhabitants of the same island. There is a community to be sought and built. Till then, this recognition is a tentative citizenship, and one big wave might wash someone away.

We agree. One has to have walked this land to appreciate the terrors of its topography – the unrelenting isolation, thoughts that spin in concentric circles, a listlessness that descends on every thought and situation, and a mind that is perfecting the art of naysaying and self-loathing. It feels as if there is nothing one can do to either escape or endure this.

Trying to help a depressed person is like trying to stop being depressed – it cannot be done, it can only be lived, while all the time hoping to surmount its invisibility.

My father drank to make it visible. And he still would not acknowledge it as depression, and he never wanted it treated. This is the nature of the illness. Like a giant coiled python that nobody can see but you, crushing your bones, swallowing you whole, and then melting you down to nothing. This is how it was for me, for three years in my thirties, but one never thinks of it as over, only as receded, and it doesn't matter what medical science has to say about it.

That is why, to be silent, I tell myself, would be to collude with the collective denial and discomfort about mental illness. I learnt this about child abuse as well – the most valuable advice is to talk about it, to tell someone, and even though the telling is just a start, it is needed. Otherwise, the shame is muted and the muted stays shameful, slowly snuffing out one's spirit. This is why one writes a memoir. This is why one tells strangers. We carry the invisible, and perhaps the telling can honour it, make it real and seen.

The Long Dying

When one has a nearly thirteen-year-old arthritic Labrador under one's care, ageing visibly by the day, health problems and visits to the vet increasing in frequency, death is but one long stride away. The symptoms were disquieting, but not much different from other symptoms over the past year. It took two days to even realize that this was not another bout of the regular ageing troubles that took us to the vet so often. And it took yet another day for the vet to diagnose that it was acute renal failure. Chinna was dying.

It was like the ghost of my father had turned up in the house.

Blood-stained stools, blood in sputum, and complete inability to eat – Chinna had all the symptoms SGM did in the weeks leading to his death, seventeen months earlier, and I tried not to think of this as a sign. I knew that Chinna had stayed with me as long as she could, that I had learnt nothing about death by turning up to touch the feet of my father's corpse and donating it to the medical college, and that this was going to be about my own mortality.

Years ago, Chinna had kept me in the world, with every ounce of canine resolution she could muster. It was into her furry shoulders that I had sobbed my pain over the loss of two pregnancies, children I was not fated to have, when she had let me curl up on the floor beside her, not moving for hours, as I bled, big chunks of me dissolving into wordless, lightless burrows.

She had watched over me day and night, sitting by my bedside while I tossed alone on the high seas of depression in an empty house. She had followed me each time to the balcony of the high-rise apartment as if she knew I wanted to jump. And then that one unforgettable night with all those pills, that night when I was perfectly aligned with death, when all it meant was release from an infernal fatigue, she had fought me with all her might.

And now it was my turn to fight for her. Perhaps, if SGM had listened to us, taken adequate action at the right time, medical science could have offered him some way to live long enough to experience old age. But there was nothing veterinary science could do, one was told, to help Chinna at that stage of her illness.

It had been three years since N had moved in to live with Chinna and me, and we had completed a circle of love I had not imagined would ever come my way. The only regret we had about getting married in a temple was that we could not take Chinna with us, but she had been waiting at the door when we had returned, our excitement reflected in her eyes. It was the ripening of the arduous journey that Chinna and I had made towards happiness, even as we knew she would not be with us for long.

N and I talked about it. Chinna had always been a very stoic and patient dog, and now she seemed to have braced herself for the full impact of this last crisis. We wanted to be brave for her, draw from her strength. We encircled her. Isn't this how dying happened in the old days, we told each other, long before ambulances turned up to whisk people off to intensive care units? People got old, they stopped eating as their organs slowed down, turned so weak that they were confined to their beds and slowly ebbed away into lifelessness. This was how one died of old age, while loved ones extended care and sat in vigil. The dying and the living had to make the transition together, and it was a one-way passage – things would change for all of us irreversibly.

Chinna stopped eating entirely. Drinking water too

was becoming difficult. For a dog always clamouring to eat, who loved to clean up every crumb, whether on the floor or her bowl, it was unthinkable, this long starvation. Her kidneys were shutting down. She could no longer pee. She retched the blood and phlegm that gurgled in her throat. She had to poop often, but what was coming out was her innards, dense bloody pieces. She lost weight every single day, her black fur hung loose around her, her eyes watery and sad. She got very little sleep and we stayed up with her, day and night, N and I. Every day I thought, this is the day, she is going to die today, but Chinna was a resilient dog and she wanted to be around us. Late in the nights, after painful bouts of vomiting blood, she would totter to my side of the bed and I would sit on the floor beside her. She put her head in my lap, and I sang to her for hours while she drew shallow breaths. With every note I felt wave after wave of love pour over her, pour out of her. She lay still, listening, my tears lapping us both.

If dogs have a sense of death and dying, how must it be? The previous year, I had failed SGM in the last weeks of his life, turned my heart away from acknowledging his fears of dying. I could not possibly do the same again with Chinna – I would be there till the end, with all my energies focused on her, about that I was determined.

Chinna had loved poetry, our daily prayer, any kind of rhythmic chanting, responding each time to cadence in words. That week that she lay dying, there were no boundaries of time, neither of sun nor of moon, nor the inching of clocks. We stayed around her, took turns to read to her, recited stories and poems about dogs, shared long passages from our prayer books and from ancient texts that had sustained us. We took turns to read and Chinna always listened intently. Was she in pain? One vet said yes, the other said no. I only trusted my instincts – I had mothered her for long years, and my heart said she wanted to still be with me, that the suffering was still manageable, that she was not ready to leave. For five days, we formed a close circle – I sang, read poetry, caressing her, talking to her about love, and finally understanding something of how low and long the spirit stretches for the dying of a beloved.

~

G the writer thought of the name Chinna because it was an endearment in Kannada, because it reminded her of her distant home during those years in Delhi where they first met. Chinna was just about eight weeks old, and G was trying to salvage her first marriage with a dog, the way she had known others to do by having a child, for she had always loved dogs and the idea seemed to cheer up a husband stressed at work. G had visited many dog owners and considered many pups, all Labradors, for she was sure of the breed, but none of them had felt like hers. But Chinna shared a birthday, 21 December, with the grandmother that G adored, and Chinna did the choosing. G had settled down on the floor to watch two puppies play so that a choice could be made, and Chinna came straight to her, climbed into her lap and showed no inclination to move, while the other puppy frolicked around. It was decided.

Chinna was a dog of calm. She did not bark at all in the first year of her life, and after that just a bark or two every year. Following a brief puppyhood of separation anxieties and the usual puppy mischief, she settled into an expansive sagaciousness. She was threatened by nobody – not other snarling dogs, nor mocking cats. She would not hurt an ant, if she could help it, and she looked at every creature, every person in her path, as a friend. Contained, patient, sensitive to sorrow in others, Chinna was the perfect writer's dog, content to sit near a busy keyboard for hours, turning silence into art.

G was with Chinna for the first three years of her nearly thirteen years' lifetime, and then again for the last four years. In between, they were apart, and even though Chinna was with family and well cared for, the separation was excruciating. It must have broken both their hearts, those six years, but G felt certain she had no other option. If G had not walked out, G would have died – that was a fact.

And Chinna wanted G to live. She taught her to live, to love, as only she could love, with the kind of enveloping, arabesque devotion that rises like incense smoke.

Their friend said he had never known two beings that kept each other at the centre of their awareness as these two did. Chinna knew every emotion that inched its way across G even before the latter could give it a name, noticing even the slightest change in the tone of her voice or the pace of her breath, and G thought she heard the softest of doggy thought. A beautiful pairing.

Then came trouble. G had turned thirty that year. She felt mismatched with her partner – it was like endless walking through arid shifting dunes – but she had her work, and she was spending hours at the National Archives trying to understand an eighteenth-century world she wanted to write about. Routine kept the marriage, like all other things, going from one weekend to the next. But in a matter of a few weeks, the wheel overturned. An unexpected pregnancy, chaos in the relationship, the tides rising as high as the skies and no anchoring whatsoever, plus a deep sense of abandonment. Even with the benefit of distance, it is hard to tell what came first, whether the black tide was the cause or the effect of those crucial decisions that had to be taken.

It was a monolith solitude, completely impenetrable.

There was a monstrous weight in her, banging against her bones, her sinews, imploding, screaming to be let out. There was a man around her saying, I never want to be a father, I never want to be a father. I don't want this father, I don't want this father, she heard a voice implore repeatedly. I never wanted you, I never wanted you, she heard her father tell a little sister.

There is no harder decision. It was no decision at all, just the dots that turned up to be joined, a line, a circuit, when all else had dissolved. Lying on her back on a hard surface, the lights of the hospital in her eyes, she heard a voice enunciate in her consciousness, I am going to have an exceptional life. Unannounced, in that moment of abject desolation, Life had turned up to whisper an encouragement. And then, it fell silent again.

It was a free fall, and there were no nets, no harnesses – only a blur of doctors, hospital beds, cold implements, colder stares, and that big haemorrhaging hole that she had turned into. As life bled out of her, a black sticky tar was replacing it, filling up rapidly, sometimes violently spinning for hours. It was getting harder to sleep or stop crying or sit up or get out of bed. At one point, it felt impossible to breathe.

The man was there, he was gone, he was back – one lost track of time. Just a large empty apartment with strange slants of light, dark memories that lurked in corners, and a self-loathing that was like a flooding tub, claiming every inch of dry space. She watched television as much as she could, she walked the dog, she ate and drank, she perfected the art of lying in bed for hours and hours without sleeping. There was no sleep at all, just brief snatches of hallucinatory wanderings of the mind. She learnt to hate herself in as many shades as it was possible to hate.

She stood, one foot lifted, on a road that did not loop, and she knew it. The phone had become a prehistoric instrument, completely obsolete – it never rang and she did not call anyone. She had learnt that people she knew judged more viciously than strangers, but maybe they were never friends, just judgements. A few years later she would emerge from the horror, she would recover, she would learn to live in her skin, she would figure out how to meet people of her tribe, how to build a new community, how to believe in the miracles of survival. But at that point, there was just Chinna, and G was tottering at the edge of the precipice.

There is nothing to keep me in the world, she thought. I hesitate to swat flies or roaches, but I gorged out what was dearest to me. There never was any childhood space to retreat into, and now I am told to be undeserving of motherhood. And I feel undeserving of everything. Why stay? Nobody needs me.

Except …

There was a two-year-old black dog right by the bed, her snout a few inches away from G's face, watching, with melting mustard-coloured eyes. Chinna's puppyhood was over, her face turned sapient. There was nobody in the house but the two of them. Chinna learnt to sleep when G slept, woke the instant she did, licked her face when she cried, shadowed her every step, countering human bleakness with animal warmth. She willed G to life.

They made it through those days, one week, one month, and then a few more.

Nothing was larger than guilt, only hope, and it made G scramble for another chance, perhaps to fix it all somehow. There was an intrepid wind of possibilities around them, some prospect of return.

Chinna was there at the door of the bathroom when the home pregnancy kit showed up positive again. G's sister was going to have her first baby as well, and the air was celebratory, with much talk of new beginnings. The benevolence of the universe was palpable, just the possibility that one could forget, start all over again. We are being given another chance, G whispered in Chinna's ears, but some mornings later she woke up to heavy bleeding, again. And again, it was just the two of them in the house. G called a friend who drove her to the hospital. After the doctor was done, G cried in the car all the way home, called the family to let them know.

God is punishing you, said G's mother.

True, G felt punished.

You are unlucky, like me, said her father.

Undeserving, unworthy, unlovable, unwanted, unwell.

She had been on a hormonal roller coaster, twice within the span of a few months. Dizzying. The mind survives by embalming the body. The body becomes loathsome, and the mind wanders in that cavernous enclosed space, talking to itself, talking incessantly. Inside was sure dying, but outside was talk in strange undecipherable tongues, and nothing was worth the trouble any more. This time there was shrill silence, no pounding at her bones, no obsessive thoughts, no leap of faith to take. G was being picked up and lowered deftly into a much more sinister space, a box with limited air supply, and the lid calmly sealed off. No plummeting this time, just slow suffocation.

~

One suffers depression, but one calls it by many names, traces it from many angles. However there is always a moment of recognition, a moment when the mind knows and calls itself ill, depressed. The illness gazes back.

After staying for days in the apartment, lying down most of the time, the only alternative that emerged was a return to work, to write one's way to sanity. I took a flight to Mysore, to the family, with Chinna sedated in a carrier in the cargo of the plane, bravely making this journey with me – both of us trying to look suitably recovered to family. Chinna rested under SGM's care, while I made day trips through the Mysore countryside, scrutinizing anything that was associated with Tipu Sultan, whose last war was the subject of my new book project, most often to Srirangapatna, an island wrapped by the river Kaveri. I was there one afternoon, almost evening, standing on a narrow bridge, and looking down at the rocky bed of a summer-scorched river. There it was, that strong urge to leap, a very fluid sensation, as if it were the most logical thing to do. The urge was tangible, like an object, and I held it tight for elastic moments.

The word 'suicidal' came to mind much later. At that time, it was as simple as taking one step forward – towards release, towards perfect freedom and stillness. More importantly, there was the knowledge that I would do it without hesitation.

And yet, I hesitated, held back.

What had turned up was the recognition, that I was not well, that this neatly formed thought of jumping was fatal. Helping myself and harming myself were now two identical, fused ideas.

I came home that evening and called the husband. I felt ready to go, I said, and a decision was taken to return to Delhi, to get help – the thought of leaping, having once arrived, was refusing to fade. There was no denying that I needed a psychiatrist, and the psychiatrist was sure that I needed a clinical psychologist as well. The misery now had a name – clinical depression.

This was new, this starting to think in terms of pills, and of time framed by visits to the doctor, to the therapist, and the harder work of figuring out how best to mop up the mess. It was an unearthing, an extrication of some self, any self, with the potential to be healthy, with the best chances of survival. The process appeared to be a mystery to everyone but Chinna, who continued her watch over every shade of emotion as it washed over me. She was changing, growing with me. At one end was Chinna, at another end was a large-hearted sister whose loyalty had room for me even as she was going through a pregnancy that required rest, and at some other end was B, a new friend with an unconditional empathy that had no precedence for me. I dangled precariously from the strands of their love, from the belief that they wanted me around, even when I was ready to go.

B said in that quiet, knowing way: You are the strongest woman I know.

How? How? I blubbered into a fresh wave of crying. I am a weepy mess and have done everything wrong and now lie shattered in a million shards – what was possibly strong about that?

B insisted with great confidence: There is nobody as tough as you, as gifted.

Months later, when I met a wise woman up in the hills, she said that the strong ones struggle the most, maybe because they question, they resist the currents, almost always they put up a fight. It sounded right at that time. Was suicide an act of courage then? Few things had made such perfect sense to me as the right to choose one's own death, but of course it could not be done under duress, or because there was no other option.

The panorama of Himalayan peaks on the wall of the corridor leading to the clinical psychologist's office always held my eye. I lingered, stealing minutes, before I entered. The sessions were expensive for someone who had turned a full-time writer and made no money, but the husband was paying, and I knew I would not be able to afford the sessions once the marriage folded. The support and direction I received in that room was incomparable. I always took my shoes off when I sat on the chair, legs folded under me, and there was finally a safe space, even if just for an hour, to think about the reasons I was tottering at the edge of the world, and not just be swallowed up by the tottering. The greatest fear, I was starting to see, was of having messed up, of being a failure – just the very thing that my father's life, my entire childhood, had been about.

But. I did not have to live my father's life. That was a revelation. I did not have to succeed in anything the way he had wanted for me, winning neither public applause nor family approval. I would fail on my own watch, at my own beat, and that was fine. The immediate crisis was as much in my head as it was about my marriage.

There were now two versions. The husband's version, which he was entitled to, had several sympathetic listeners, including many in the family, while I had decided to keep my privacy, and not even my own parents were told what had transpired. I had chosen to marry this man and now the consequences were mine to bear. This present telling too is a tapestry of gaps, trying to stay with moments as I experienced them.

I begged the psychologist to intervene. Controlling, critical personalities never see or accept that they are being controlling or critical, please tell him to stop.

She agreed to see us together. There were too many words in that room that day, and I was feeling that unendurable fatigue again. He was explaining, and my gut was caving in – those same phrases, those same distances.

At one point, we were asked, how is the marriage working for you?

He thought it was great, said he would give it eight, maybe even nine, out of ten.

I held up two digits of one hand.

How was it possible that we were in the same marriage? This is so wrong, I thought.

The treatment, a mix of antidepressants and therapy sessions, started in May or June 2005, and by September there was no doubt about what had to be done. So simple, so unassailable, and yet it had never occurred to me before – walk away from the hurtful, the unfair, walk towards the open spaces.

But I had no strength to walk. Only a shell remained. Inside was a tempest of sorrows and regrets, and a drowning in tears that allowed no field of vision.

I was all set for a quiet exit from life, unwilling to turn thirty-two, and I was entirely at peace with that knowledge. The medicines were dutifully taken, therapy sessions attended. But what stretched ahead were the endless minutes that made each day and night, the complete pointlessness and mockery of getting through those minutes too evident to ignore. Those days, weeks, are now a smear, and I can't place things in chronological order with even the remotest surety. The pills that helped me sleep were addictive, but the sleep was not restful. The only thing that undid the constant knot in the chest was a drink in the evenings, but that was a terrible thing to mix with pills and made things worse. The days felt unbearably long, the nights even more so, and I felt trapped in a cage of skin and bones, constantly felt that I was the wrong person, wrong in every way.

SGM, who had been self-medicating with alcohol, had not only perfected the art of denial, but was used to casting his illness in heroic terms. His drinking, his dark spells, had to be emblematic of his strong spirit that fought adverse events and endured destiny. This was how he talked about it. To then have a daughter with a diagnosis of depression, with any hint of mirroring his own situation, was tricky. For once, it was not about him, and why a capable child like me was floundering was an equal mystery. He preached on the phone about strength of mind, about suicide being entirely an act of cowardice. He said about himself, look at me, I am not a coward. Think positive, have faith in God, said my mother. These speeches remained all that my parents did for their depressed child that year. There was no question of visiting or caretaking, nor did I expect it – with no such precedent even in impressionable years, it could not happen now or ever.

We all need something to live for, and what I had was Chinna and my writing, but even those could not balance out the daily slow dying, and I made my plan. I sent an email saying my goodbye to the husband who was then in another country, another time zone where I felt certain the mail would not be read for hours. The soul felt light, ready for flight.

But the email had been read instantly, my sister contacted, and my brother-in-law was on a flight to get to our house before I was gone. I knew none of this, and was set – pills of various sizes gathered in a bowl and a drink on the dining table.

And then Chinna started to jump at me, like she never had before or since, again and again. Jumping and pushing my arm, ignoring my rebukes, thrusting her paws on my chest, she fought me till the doorbell rang.

~

One drastic act had to replace another, no matter how small it might be on the scale of things. A death wish had been set in motion and there was only one way to stop it. Perhaps an alternative of sorts, to mimic it in the least harmful way but make sure it hurts – sharp enough to leave an imprint.

I want to cut my hair short, G told the psychiatrist, but I am afraid I will regret it.

She had long hair, thick and cascading down to her thighs, almost to her knees. It was her pride, an important part of her self-image, of how she knew others saw her – the long-haired girl. Naturally, it had to go now.

The doctor looked up from his desk, puzzled. He had not even noticed that she had long hair, but he had taken the trouble to read her novel, and he always held her gaze intently, the look of true listening. Finding a good match with one's psychiatrist and psychologist in this country where mental illness is woefully underserved is like winning the lottery, and G had been lucky with both.

Your hair, your regret, the doctor said, shrugging. That sounded right to her. And soon she was with a hairstylist. The scissors at her nape, the crisp crunching of its blade on a thick cluster of hair, the fall, the lightness. It was over.

Fresh starts don't happen with hair, not really. Nothing changed. It was the same apartment, the same sense of worthlessness, only more unbearable with each passing day.

They tried a holiday and took Chinna along, a long drive into the heights of Kumaon. There was a table by a window from where G could see a golden outline of snow-draped peaks. She tried to write about what happened, but the anxieties were returning with greater frequency, with higher intensity, and even the medicines were barely helping. Talking about mental illness with someone who stands outside its draining power is not just frustrating but further damaging. She coiled. There was beauty wherever one looked – tall cedar trees, meandering streams, a wild waterfall, and Chinna to share it all with. But the dog was starting to act worried. She never let G out of her sight, not if she could help it.

Lying in a hammock, Chinna curled up below it, G tried to pretend there was no time before or after, just that windfall of quiet. She was alive and that was all there was to it. But all this only till the next wave of grief rose in her. The chest would turn into a hard knot, no air entering or escaping from it, and the heart would start to push out against the ribcage and push into the stomach, turning harder, darker, knottier. The anguish grew as high as those looming peaks and all felt bleak, especially when they returned to the plains, to the city, back to the apartment with its pale walls, pale floor and memories of deep injustice.

G thought a lot about what it meant to desire life, and what the absence of that desire entailed. Where she stood in the tunnel, its deepest point, there was a curve and she could not see the lit circles at either end, not even dots of light. It did not help that one day, returning from a therapy session, her autorickshaw was in an accident, and the sharp pain in her neck turned out to be whiplash. She was back to being unable to take care of herself and whatever was expected in the house. She stopped reading or writing. She could not bear the sight of the double bed and slept on the couch.

The television ran for hours. Chinna hovered obsessively again. Not a good sign.

Akka, come home, I am sending you an air ticket, her sister said. First that doorbell, and now this ticket – her life was drawn back from the edge yet again.

There was treatment and rest and loving care in her sister's house in Bangalore. Nothing could possibly make G return to that apartment again, only Chinna, but then there would be a price to pay, perhaps the only one that really mattered, the one that was still beating in her chest. She lay down beside her pregnant sister, trying to feel the presence of the new life, wondering if it would be a niece or nephew, wondering if she would be around long enough to see it all happen.

SGM came to visit – G's parents had known nothing of what had happened, they believed marriages were meant to last – and a pointless conversation ensued. He tried to persuade her to go back to the husband, and she told him she would be dead if she did. He pottered around the garden in numbed silence and returned by the evening train to Mysore.

SGM did not ask G to come home. He did not ask what she might need to get back on her feet. He just hoped that circumstances would force his daughter to return to her marriage. All these years of fathering a wilful child, shaping her in his ideals, his aspirations for her were entirely for professional fame, the personal assumed to be taking care of itself. The possibility that his child would end up with nothing, no profession and no family, was unthinkable. He had failed in his life yet again, or so he said as he sank into his rum.

G declared there was no option but to walk away from the marriage, but there was still Chinna to think about. What could she do? She had no money or a roof to call her own, and a big dog needed its routine and care.

Forgive me, G told Chinna, forgive me for leaving. But this will help me live, start again, and I know you want that. But Chinna was too engrossed in the new squeaky toys that G had brought her that evening to pay attention to what was happening. Two bags of clothes were packed, along with one box of books that G could not live without, the credit cards and house keys were put down on the table. She was ready to leave. All of her life reduced to two suitcases, very little money in the wallet and nothing in the bank – this would be her life for a long time but she did not know how long. There was no room to think or feel – one just had to act as if one were in a building on fire. A longer plan than heading for the exit was impossible, nor did it matter then.

It was late in the evening. A friend came and took the box of books. The rest she hauled into an autorickshaw and went over to stay with another friend, but only for a few days. Soon, a small job in some office, a bed in a hostel space that was the size of her old closet, and that piercing ache for her beloved dog – it was trial by fire.

She was told about this mud house in the foothills of the Dauladhar range, built by a maverick artist who needed someone to watch house and dog for a few weeks. G decided to go. She felt better, and she felt she was going to be well again. First the therapy sessions stopped, then the medication. There was some money coming in from a freelance writing job, and with no family home to return to, it felt right to burrow into the ageless hills, to recover among strangers. It was a gift from the heavens – she could take shelter in a beautiful little village in Himachal Pradesh, a short drive from Dharamshala, learn to feel the shape of the earth as she went on long walks, find pleasure again in cooking, in watching clouds, in gathering flowers for a little vase on a mud sill.

It sounds idyllic, and it was, but depression knows no spatial boundaries, it resists naive notions of clean starts. The earth kept appearing and disappearing under G's feet. She was writing when she could, and there were beautiful people around her, sublime moments in nature, another book at the printers, the possibility of returning to academics by going abroad the following year, the birth of an angelic niece, the freedom to rediscover forgotten pleasures. But the dark clots returned, spread. The horizon was joyless, dying slowly again. She resumed medication, tried homeopathy this time, and the body reacted in strange ways, like a buoy on choppy waters.

Her body. She crawled in it. She had always hated it. It had a knack for looking 'normal' and she hated it even more for that. Till she was hurrying down the steps of a department store during a visit to the city, and her eyes stopped at a string of brightly coloured baby shoes, each clinging to its twin, awaiting tiny baby feet. Everything turned intensely black, all but the baby shoes. A fine blade was slicing her open, turning her inside out. A body crammed with childhood screams. It was a tidal wave straight from the marrow. She tumbled out of the store, and it was night.

Back in the hills, people around her showered love and care that she accepted with gratitude, even loved back. Normal was easy again. There was so much to do – apply for a visa, move again to the plains, get everything organized. The body was slowing down, but the mind had to keep marching, and there was no time to think till one got to foreign shores. Perhaps the dark clouds would not migrate that far.

~

Is suffering like this inherited? Or does one gather it along the way? I am in Wales, living a few yards away from the River Tawe that swirls in dense blue circles. It looks less like water to me, more like smeared oil paints, and late in the nights when I am crawling out of my skin, the river calls me, calls me to itself. I imagine what the sinking will feel like, the first contact with the water, the closing of those thick watery curtains over my head. I am tempted but I try to close my eyes, each time I try not to listen to the river calling my name.

What should I do? How could someone else comprehend if no river had spoken to them like this? I call home, and my father is not surprised by my questions.

What was your father like? Was he conflicted, withdrawn into his own darkness? I had never met my grandfather – he had died of a stroke in his late forties or early fifties, and was known to be a man of few words and great temper.

Yes.

Do you think you are like your father?

Yes.

I don't need to ask if I am like him. We have already been through that, several times over. My grandfather was distinct, I have been told, talented in many ways, and so was my father. Why aren't we talking about that? We just don't. My father is relieved the daughter is in foreign lands, getting more degrees – it is something he talks about to anyone who will listen. To me he says, forget the past, start afresh.

There is no staying away from the river as I cycle against blustering winds to get to the university. All the Welsh I have known are effusively warm and it is an easy place to feel perennially loved, for even the checkout lady at the supermarket thinks your name is 'luv' or 'lovely' and you know something of that is genuinely meant. Everything is an enticing curve in the town – the river, the roads, the beach, the foliage. I understand what it means to be embedded in the landscape. The high cliffs of Pennard are like geological manifestations of my deepest desires, the air has the sweet scent of flowers, the hillside is dotted with the lush gold of daffodils that have only been a poem to me till then, and the rains sweep in from the bay with unmitigated passion. It is the finest place to feel the pulse of life beat in oneself, but the river was still calling my name, and this time it had nothing to do with marriage or death. There was the pain of parting from Chinna, but that was not it – something else was afoot. That inky tar that had earlier told me I was irreparably flawed and that life was not worth any of its troubles still had roots, still drew sustenance from unresolved nooks, and it was sprouting dark shoots.

To make things harder, the divorce proceedings had started in Delhi in my absence, and I spoke to the judge on Skype. Sure, I have no objection. The lawyer authorized to sign for me had been found by the husband who wanted the divorce and I had asked for nothing.

You should sue for emotional trauma, said my father. He consulted some lawyer and apparently I had a case.

There is nothing in the world that could possibly compensate for what I went through, I don't care, I said. Maybe if he could give Chinna back to me?

The answer to that was a no, because she was now with his aged parents who had grown very attached to her.

Any email now from the man was an aggravation of an intense kind.

Fine, let us get on with the paperwork. Legal

paperwork, those insufferable signatures and attestations and notaries and powers of attorneys, journeys to the Indian consulate in London and back, the spirit being wrung dry. So finally when the judge said, madam, please tell us if you have any objections, what could I say? That I did not deserve to have suffered so much? That the marriage had died long ago for me, and this was just a courtroom setting him free from any legal obligations to me? And anyway, what did legal obligations mean when one had failed morally? Yes, this divorce was acceptable to me.

I shut the computer, stood up and looked at myself in the mirror. My hair was growing out in strange ways, a straggly bush, and long streaks of grey had emerged where there were none the previous month. I had weathered in days. Whatever reserves of energy had been gathered and drawn from sparingly were steadily depleting.

B came visiting. He had taken over the protective watch from Chinna, mostly through daily communication across continents, and I kept no secrets from him. He waited patiently as I sobbed inconsolably for hours, then announced in his usual kind but firm way that this needed taking care of immediately. The Gujarati doctor on the local NHS (National Health Service) circuit looked deeply disappointed that a young Indian woman had mental health difficulties, and that an older American man accompanied her.

Indians are tough, they adjust anywhere, and finding some way to be part of the local Indian community would cure of me these blues, he was sure of that.

Just write me a reference to a psychiatrist, I said. I was a veteran now, and it was clear I had to get back on the SSRI pills.

Like nearly everyone else I know who has dealt with anxieties or depression, I resisted and disliked taking these anti-depressants. I fought against medication as much as I could when it was first mentioned to me. One feels as if one has admitted to weakness or defeat when one takes medicines to fix some strange sounding chemicals in the brain that can miraculously cause or stop our suffering. Even as one is taking the medicines, the first few weeks are wretched – there is very little benefit and plenty of side effects, not easy when one is already feeling like a trash can. Then one notices that the weepy bouts are much reduced, and there is some semblance of a sleep cycle, and perhaps the pills are finally helping the body cope. One also notices that just as plunging sorrows are getting removed from one's system, soaring joys are also gone, and all emotions now fall in a narrow, albeit stable band in the middle. One struggles to find the right word to describe that medicated space – not quite numbness, almost wooliness, and the awareness that one is not quite oneself, like the gap we are told to mind between the train and the platform. Yet, this thin middling band in an emotional quagmire becomes the first step towards sanity.

Getting on the medication was easier than getting a therapist on the NHS. I was told the waiting list was too long. I couldn't go back to my previous therapist, trying the Skype route, because after ending our professional relationship, I had asked for us to be friends and she had agreed with some reservations. We did not talk about the therapy sessions and it was a friendship that I wanted very much to keep. So now I found myself directed to an NHS website that had put together CBT (cognitive behavioural therapy) modules for beginners. I was no beginner at this but I was willing to do whatever it takes. I was as weary of relapses as of the illness itself. I printed booklets and workbooks from the website, some of which felt like elementary platitudes, but I knew they were working away at something, at old ways of thinking, encouraging new survival skills, and I did the exercises obsessively, day after day.

I had learnt my lesson and was not going to take chances with the medication, and the CBT taught me something – a happier life was already within my orbit of possibilities. I just had to go about it in certain other ways. I could be anything I wanted to be. All words of self-deprecation and self-loathing in one's head were entirely a perspective, a trick of light. One has to simply change that, look at it all a little differently, talk back to that negative voice with verve, and the wheel starts to turn in ways that sync with our best selves. But it was agonizingly slow – I cannot lie. And there were too many moments of doubts and despair. It was yet another long slog through yet another long curved tunnel.

Just as there is the moment of recognition, when the self defines the mental illness, there is such a thing as an awareness of recovery. It would take two more years, of medication and CBT, I would have moved to yet another continent, and even though there were equally stressful life events to handle then, I found myself in the direction of recovery. I have no explanation for why this did not happen before or why it was happening then. This was at the end of 2008. And there hasn't been a relapse since.

~

Depression or not, productivity was never a problem for her. Work always got done, almost always ahead of time.

Sometimes she felt she wrote her best in the deepest trough of the depression, almost as if to keep moving through the days. The idea of dying and leaving behind an incomplete manuscript haunted her. She hurried to finish, worked like a maniac, barely slept.

Her academic journey in the UK had to be shorter than planned, and she moved, with the incomplete manuscript and the pills, to the United States, where she had received a teaching assistantship for a doctoral degree. This would turn out to be the space for her new anchoring, but in her was a growing craving for the heat, the colour, the chaos of distant home.

I want to quit, go back, I do not belong here, she said to the Graduate Chair in the first weeks at the university.

Look at this pile here, he said, all these people applied, did not make it here, but you got through. Think about it, he said.

Maybe she should stay. But could she get done sooner, leave before her five years of assistantship was over?

Yes, if all the work was done, why not?

She was now teaching classes regularly to undergraduates, as energetic and fraught as only young adults can be, and in the compassion she felt for them, she also found some compassion for her own broken younger self. It was the beginning of her first Midwest winter, the first layers of snowfall quietly settling in for long frozen grey months, and in her palm was the last pill she would take. She had run out of her stock of medicines and the only way to get more was to find a new doctor in a new country. She decided to go off the medication, join yoga classes, surround herself with every book she could find on the science of happiness, listen to every talk on positive psychology by leading experts.

What depression meant to her grandfather, and what it meant to her father – not an illness, not a terminology, only a cluster of despairings and untimely deaths – was not going to be what it meant to her. By now she was looking at her depression as if it were a fellow traveller in an adjoining berth on a long train journey – they sized each other up, they talked tentatively, they stayed wary and affable at the same time. She felt its breath on her nape when she took long walks through the tall grass prairie, when she was cooking elaborate feasts entirely for herself in her little kitchen, when she learnt to dance the tango, when she sang in languages nobody around her could understand. Between her and depression were the kinds of boundaries that lovers in new relationships valiantly try to put in place.

Even an unavoidable surgery in a foreign country, without any caregivers or family support, except for kind visiting friends, was a reminder that one was grateful for life. She discovered pleasure in work, gathered courage to open her heart, learnt the art of friendship, slowly grew into her skin, in a way for the first time. She was even inhaling and exhaling differently – or maybe the winds had changed direction. An excerpt of her dissertation manuscript won an award for creative writing although its real triumph had been to keep her afloat when large parts of her were dying, and the department thought she deserved an award for teaching too. The days felt delicately bountiful. It was time to go home.

The real reward was to come a few months after her return. Chinna was now nine years old, and even though G had not seen her since she had walked out of that apartment six years ago, she had never given up hope that they would be reunited. The ex-husband was getting married again – good luck to them – and his parents wanted someone else to take care of Chinna in her old age.

Of course, I will take her. Yes, yes, yes.

The date was fixed to receive Chinna. G had no home of her own and her parents had to agree to the plan. SGM, who could not bear to see any animal suffer and was the patron saint of all canines in his neighbourhood, worried about how she would manage the care of a big old dog when her plans were still in flux, but he agreed.

Chinna is yours. You should take her back. But the price of this loving is too great, it is heartbreaking, think about it, he proclaimed in a gloom-laden tone.

In the recent past, he had found a white Labrador on his usual walk in the colony. The dog had been abandoned to die. Nobody knew who had left it there and its state was pitiful. SGM brought it home, called the vet who confirmed the dog's kidneys had collapsed and that there was nothing left to do, but SGM would not give up. He kept the dog at home, nursed it for over a week, paid for expensive medicines, fervently hoped for a recovery. When the dog died, he mourned and buried it in a nearby patch of land. This nameless dying dog had been deeply loved just before its death. Perhaps I had some unsettled accounts and debts with him in a previous birth, SGM said, wiping his tears.

SGM fed street dogs for years, he gave them names, called the SPCA when they needed help, made donations for their treatment when he could, played with their puppies, made stories about them to tell everyone. There were too many tragedies as well – dogs that were poisoned or mortally wounded, or puppies that drowned in gutters. Sooner or later, nearly all his dogs were prematurely dead somehow. It is too much to bear, he often moaned to G on the phone. His own Gracy, the one who lived to be nineteen, grew a tumour and had to be put to sleep not so long ago. Gracy was buried in the garden and every day SGM missed her. He never called her his dog, always his youngest daughter, took her with him everywhere he went. Life, he found, became hardest to manage after Gracy died.

They are sending Chinna back to you as she is ageing, SGM said to G on a walk. Look how I suffered when the dogs died – is it worth it?

Yes, absolutely worth it. G would not want it any other way.

Once Chinna had dragged G back from the edge and stayed with her in the slow crawl back to life. Now it was G's turn to walk with Chinna into her old age, to stay with her through the long dying. Chinna would be the most important priority in her life for whatever doggy years she had left – some debts were too large to be repaid, but one had to try nonetheless.

The reunion was hard. Chinna jumped out of the car and ran into the house, a house that she had visited before, that clearly brought back a flood of memories. She ran to G's mother, made quick visits to all the rooms, stayed close to the people who were dropping her off, but she would not look at G who sat on the floor calling her – Chinna, Chinna. Was it a shock for Chinna to see G again after six years? Or was she angry at how G had walked out of her life and was now letting it be known? G felt wretched, her heart burst open with tears – I am sorry, I am very sorry – but Chinna would not come, and when the people who came with her left, she let out a long whine, as if she knew her life was changing course again. Perhaps she worried G would leave her again.

Walk, walk, G said the magic words as she clipped the collar to a leash, and Chinna ran out, dragging G into the grass. Their feet synced. This was familiar. Like a lost dream conjured again.

G stayed with Chinna through many days, hardly ever letting her out of sight. The reconnecting had to happen as if they were meeting for the first time, and this time the choosing, the wooing would have be done by G. In a couple of days after returning to her, Chinna looked less anxious and more settled, especially around SGM whom she happily anointed the pack leader and followed around. Groom her, said the vet, that is the best way to bond. And that is what G did, brushing Chinna's fur, bathing her, cleaning her ears and teeth, going on long walks. Soon it was time to move away so that they could be a family again, just the two of them, to a small rented house in Bangalore where they stayed over eight months.

The first few days in Bangalore were hard. G and Chinna were cooped up in a small space, and it was clear that Chinna was anxious, and it appeared that she was missing her previous home with the ex-husband's family very much. G worked from home and stayed with Chinna nearly all the time, but Chinna would get visibly restless, would whine to herself. It was too hard for G. I should not be selfish, she thought – if Chinna does not want to be with me any more, I should return her. Just like Chinna once wanted me to be happy, I want the same for her now.

Even though every cell in her body protested, for Chinna's sake, she wrote to the other family – would they take the dog back?

No. That was the simple answer, and the explanations tagged to it did not matter.

It is going to be just us, old girl, G told Chinna. And we will make it work. It will be okay.

G's sister came to their rescue again. There were now two young ones in the family – a niece and a nephew – and they all lived not far from G and Chinna. The children doted on Chinna and she was happy to let them fuss on her, climb on her, tug at her. She slipped into her old age effortlessly, became a doting grandmother to the kids.

There was no more anxiety or whining. They were finally together for whatever lay ahead.

The geriatric challenges had already begun – first arthritis, then incontinence. Chinna asked to be taken out in the middle of the night and every couple of hours, an ordeal for her and everyone, till a suitable medication was found. G lost a lot of weight for no apparent reason, and a few months later had to contend with the first sign of spondylitis. They were back to taking care of each other, strangely content in knowing they were going to wear out together. It was as if they were back to 2003 when Chinna was a pup that never let G out of her sight or sphere of awareness. It was just like that.

G knew there would not be much time with Chinna, and that the ageing would occur rapidly now. She, a habitual traveller, lost all desire to go anywhere or to visit anyone – anything that would take her away from Chinna was to be avoided. She did not want Chinna to ever feel abandoned by her. I will never leave you, she promised several times. G knew Chinna had just one more move in her, and it would have to be to a place where G had a livelihood, and they would set up a home together.

They moved to a little coastal town, to work for a university, not far from where G was born, and not far from the villages where her parents were born. It was the land that had formed SGM, the roots that he felt so conflicted about, where his daughter now chose to live with her dog. A dog-loving couple had kindly agreed to rent their beautiful lake view apartment to G and Chinna. This university town would be their last stop together, where Chinna would be buried.

~

N and I were now keeping vigil as Chinna lay dying. Even as she stopped many daily activities – eating, drinking, rolling around on the carpet for pettings – she tried her best to muster enough energy for small walks, hobbling through the overgrown grass of the vacant land next to our house, smelling earth and other creatures, lifting her nose up to catch the wind and the sunlight. She continued to keep her eye on us, wanting as always to be in the same room as us, even when she had trouble moving.

The day of the blood test, we found out that the symptoms were not due to a recurrent anal infection, or the usual indigestion, but because her kidneys were failing. We lifted and held her on the vet's table. He attached a saline water drip to her and she endured it, too weak to protest. I could see her unhappiness about being in that space, about having that liquid forced into her, and she was violently sick in the car on the way back.

The vomiting would not stop that night. I held her between the heaves, and she slept a little in the early hours of the morning. What on earth were we going to do? Yes, we had decided to stay away from work and spend all our time with her, offer the best palliative care we could at home, but we knew nothing about waiting for death, about the anguish of watching helplessly while a loved one bled.

This was Tuesday and by Thursday evening, we could tell that neither was the suffering going to abate, nor was she going to die soon. She was showing every sign of lingering, of going the excruciatingly slow, painful way. Even drinking water was becoming difficult, but she would look at our pleading eyes and take little licks from the bowl we held out. Were we being selfish in wanting to keep her with us as long as possible, wishing a natural death for her? I remember driving desperately to the house of a friend who loved dogs, banging on her gate, hoping for advice, and then calling up a doctor who had many animals under her care, who came to the rescue if any dog was in distress. What should we do? What should we do?

She will not go so easily, the doctor said. She may even take fifteen more days to waste away – do you want her to go through that? It is hard, but you have to be brave, you have to spare her the suffering.

Tell me what to do, tell me what to do, I wept, I cannot bear to see her like this.

But I could not bear to let her go either. My father must have had some idea this day would come. A vocal supporter of euthanasia, for human and animals, he had told me several times: Do not let her suffer.

The doctor gave me the number of a vet, someone she trusted, who could come home to help Chinna with her death, if and when we decided to go that way. We rushed back home, and Chinna was sitting in a corner, waiting for us. There were blotches of blood that she had pooped in different corners of the house. N and I sat on the floor, petting her, knowing we could not let her go on like this, even though my heart was protesting. The doctor and another friend dropped by to see us, and for the first time in days, Chinna got up to greet someone, her tail wagging as in the good old days. A few minutes later she was tired and went back to her bed to lie down.

That night, the blood gurgled in her throat frequently, and she threw up as much as she could, and she could no longer control the bloody diarrhoea that was coming out from her, messing her bed for the first time in her life. We mopped, kept her clean, changed sheets frequently. N was tired, and I suggested he go to sleep. But I could not sleep – I did not want to – and stayed up with her all night. She moved from one room to another, regurgitating as she stumbled on, and I followed her. When she got a little respite from the bleeding, she put her head on my lap, and I sang anything that came to mind, anything to ease the weight of the night.

Finally we moved to the living room where she had a little bed. We heard thunder. I opened the door and strong cool winds blew into the house of death. We had a thunderstorm, unseasonal and unannounced but of monsoon-like fury, large heavy raindrops hammering away at the house, the trees around us swaying fiercely, big flashes of lightening. It should have felt apocalyptic, but no, it was like the skies were soothing us, telling us it was going to be okay. Weary and miserable, I lay down on the couch where Chinna and I could see each other. I did not want to be out of her sight for even a moment. We watched the rain, both of us, breathing in tandem, a long journey of togetherness at its end.

Sometime that night, while it was raining, Chinna lifted her head with effort and looked at me, and I held her gaze. Her watery eyes spoke volumes. A sea of compassion, endurance and pain. That was the first moment I knew she was ready to go, that she could not take it any more.

At the first light of dawn, I woke N and told him about the decision. It was time to end the suffering, release this loving soul from a body that had become torturous. The doctor called us to see how the night had gone and talking to her helped us make the next phone call, to the vet who said he would be there soon. We had about an hour with Chinna who had moved into the bedroom, walking with great difficulty. I spread her freshly washed red blanket on the floor of the living room, and I told N we would have to find a way to bring her to it before the vet came. Chinna must have heard me, because in a few minutes, in a last act of staggering kindness to us, she slowly got up and walked over to the blanket and lay down near it. I put her head on my lap and N read to her from the Upanishad.

> Nachiketa asks the Lord of Death: When a man dies, this doubt arises: some say 'he is' and some say 'he is not'. Tell me the truth.
>
> Death replies: Even the Gods had this doubt in times of old – for mysterious is the law of life and death. Ask for another boon. Release me from this.

Chinna lay very still and we knew she was listening. I wanted to be brave for her. I did not want to say any words of goodbye or farewell. I had promised to never leave her again, and I did not want her to get anxious that morning. We had had a beautiful partnership and we would bring the best of offerings, our deepest selves, to this parting. Only boundless gratitude can begin to comprehend this gift lying in my lap, this gift of life and love.

I am here for you, I am here.

N continued to read in that beautiful melodic voice of his, wavering now and then but picking up each word with perfect care.

> Beyond the senses is the mind, and beyond mind is reason, its essence. Beyond reason is the Spirit in man, and beyond this is the Spirit of the universe, the evolver of all.

When the doorbell rang, we were out of time. The vet called the laboratory to get the readings of Chinna's blood test again, just to make sure. The creatinine levels were incredibly high, and this was three days ago, which meant she was in great agony now. N and I carefully lifted Chinna to the red blanket – she was limp and unresponsive – and I sat down close to her, pulling as much of her on my lap as I could. Both my arms were around her. I patted her, told her I was right there.

The vet said it would only take a few seconds. I saw the injection go in, her limbs twitched for a few seconds, and then went still. The vet said it was over, that the rigor mortis had set in, and he put his finger on her open eye to show me. No reaction. But her heart was still beating and my palm was right over her heart. Yes, there is still blood circulating in her but she is gone, the vet said. I let my palm stay there till I felt the last beat. I looked up and only when I saw N sobbing did I realize that I had stayed composed, that every ounce of courage in my body had been wrapped around her. I had kept my promise, and Chinna was now a part of me, her heart continuing to beat in mine. I had never loved this much before, and I could never love like this again. This is the sort of merging that comes our way just once in a lifetime, if we are fortunate.

I am.

After, then Before

Why don't we talk about this, you and I?

You may not see it as I do, but fathers change – it is the nature of things. We are encouraged to think about a fixed category, a man wrapped up in a role, a biological supposition, a social entanglement, Father from when the child is born till one of them dies. But you changed, as you should, as I did. It would have been a lot easier for both of us if we had just talked and agreed that there were as many fathers as there were daughters in our relationship.

When you held me for the first time, in that government hospital, you were just twenty-six years old, barely a husband for a year, and an independent man of means for a little longer than that. What could have possibly prepared you to be a father? You admired your father, but he was not around, a man who juggled detachment and passion, a man of quirks and talents, who wore out and died before he saw your children. Did you always want to be like him?

You look at me from the framed photograph near my bed, ripe with youth and confidence, your eyes intense, like bottomless pools. There are none of those ghouls that I would later spy fleeting across on your face. Back then, yours is a fearless kind of handsome, lean and charming, the flavour of which I can faintly recollect. Just twenty-six. I know that you wanted to be all that your father was, and do even better with me – you wanted a girl child, you wanted to raise her to be bold, independent, competent, and you wanted to be her friend. You tried.

At thirty-six, you were struggling to keep your faith in the workings of the world, unable to find anything to stem your inner storms except rage or some substance to numb it with. You stood at a vital crossroads then, the man I loved unquestioningly, and I was a child of ten, floundering with the weight of secrets I could not tell. You now had another daughter and any preoccupations with the art of fathering had long slipped out of your mind. In the family albums is a darkened version of the previous image, more leathery, leaner, hair and moustache thicker, eyes set deeper, but something about you has turned inscrutable. Surely I am not imagining the wall that has started to go up around you, so early, still in your thirties.

At forty-six, it was too late for both of us. I was getting ready to leave home, all your aspirations and principles loaded on my back. Both of us knew we would now have to learn to live without being the mirrors we had been to each other, and you were swapping hope for drink. I could still talk to you, and you sent little notes to me, made speeches on the phone or when we met – you did not like that I was not following your plan for me, but you tried to see my dreams, maybe dream them a little too, even when they broke.

I saw you turn the corner of middle age, just a couple of years older than I am now, your hair thinning, an alcohol-fat belly that would only grow, and all your tobacco-stained teeth pulled out to make room for dentures. How easily that indefatigable youth was giving way to a steady erosion, even as everyone confidently said that yours was the heart that would stay forever young – the consummate entertainer, always, my father, you continued to exude the lustre of a falling star.

At fifty-six, it was stormy weather. You had walked away from a job that kept you at work all day to an unknown that could only be buoyed by alcohol, and you were already talking about the end, about death, about a world rapidly deteriorating beyond salvage. The wait for the highly successful daughter was starting to look like one more heartbreak to endure. You were scanning the skies, but I was not flying. I was tucked away in a faraway nest, using words to probe and own solitary spaces. You were on your own now, as was I. Both of us had known the horrors of chronic sadness. Where could we go from here? What chance did we have?

At sixty-six, you were dead.

All photographs of your fifties and sixties are going to lie to me, I cannot look. You were slowly poisoning yourself, with sorrow, with tobacco, with drink. Your belly would bloat with the poisons, the rest of you would shrink, your hair entirely white, your skin lifeless, and that pain, that suffocation in your eyes, as you turned away from us, as you talked about dying, about disappointment, about anger and frustration. Everything you mourned played on your face when you talked – without your knowledge, the toxins were quietly taking over.

In your last decade, it was not me, your child of promise, but your other daughter who would be there for you and your wife. She would be the one to stay close, visit often, arrange for medical treatment, form the backup cavalry to your household. You complained about taking favours, you did not thank her when you should have, but you were grateful for her, you saw her differently, you even shared your feelings with her, that one time during a car ride when you cried to her about your loneliness. All the pictures of your last years have been taken by her.

When your grandchildren arrived, I admit that I worried. Would that old flash of temper show, would that hand swing impulsively, would there be those hard words again? But being a grandfather, I saw with amazement, was not the same as being a father. You were delighted. You tried to be a delight. Your granddaughter, my precious niece, may have been reticent, not the outgoing child you could parade around to your friends, but you beamed radiant love, one could not deny that. It was a little different when the grandson came. This time, you really caved in, grew obsessively attached to that little fellow, probably remembering how your grandfather had once adored you. Our worries stayed. Why lift the child when you are still under the influence of alcohol? Why insist on taking him on scooter rides when your hands constantly shake? You are adamant, proud, completely devoted to his every whim. You are his Ajja, and he has your flair for showmanship.

You pick him up, a month-old baby, settle down in a chair by a window, hold him close to your chest, cradle him in your arms and smile down at him as he smiles in his sleep. It is a world occupied only by the two of you. Your daughter's camera is gazing at you but you are probably not aware. Ensconced in the photograph, after so many years, is that same old calm, that containment, which was there in your twenty-six-year-old self. It is momentary, this look and feeling, and it will leave, but I am glad it emerged from some long forgotten alleys of life, one last time. Perfect poise, perfect calm, a complete love.

I imagine … this is how you must have looked when you picked up an infant me, and held me close to your chest …

No, not imagine, I do remember – just this one nugget of memory …

Years ago, I had described the scene to my mother, every little detail and sensation, and this was before there were computers and televisions in our lives, so we had to agree that those images had no other source but my memory.

You cannot possibly remember, my mother said, but we had taken you to the Vivekananda Rock Memorial in Kanyakumari. What you describe seems to be that visit. You were just a year old then. It cannot be.

But it can be, because I distinctly recollect a space and a light. A room with large well-lit windows that open